More Precious than Gold

More Precious than Gold

BASILEA SCHLINK

Creation House
Carol Stream, Illinois

Copyright © Basilea Schlink, 1978
Original Title: *Er redet noch*
First German Edition — 1968

Originally published by Marshall, Morgan & Scott, London, 1978.

United States edition published in 1978 by Creation House,
499 Gundersen Drive, Carol Stream, Illinois 60187
Distributed in Canada: Beacon Distributing Ltd., 104 Consumers Drive,
Whitby, Ontario LIN 5T3

ISBN 0-88419-178-8
Library of Congress Catalog Card Number (Applied for)
Printed in the United States of America

More Precious than Gold

A Present for Every Single Day of the Year!

Each day this book brings us a precious gift of God in the form of a Scripture text and a challenge from our Lord, who still speaks to us today. We shall be astonished to see the wide variety of commandments the Lord has given us in both the Old and the New Testament. Indeed, the Ten Commandments, given on Mount Sinai, shine forth anew in the New Testament. In the commandments God has revealed His heart to us. He has shown us what moves His heart and what He desires of us. And in fulfilling His requests, we shall bring joy to Him, and peace will fill our hearts.

The brief explanatory texts are designed to help us to understand the rousing call contained in the commandments, but more than that, to appreciate the offer of God's love expressed in them. God in His love desires our happiness. In giving us the commandments, He has shown us how to attain this happiness, and that is by loving Him and our neighbour. If we practise genuine love, we shall become happy and also make others happy. All the commandments are either a call to love or are a warning against actions contrary to love, such as murder, theft, adultery, slander. In short, the commandments are intended to keep us from sinning against love.

The commandments of love are a great gift for us, but they are also holy. And it is of utmost importance that we cherish them and hold them sacred. We cannot simply do with them as we please. The commandments of God stand like solid rock. Though we may try to undermine them, they will not fall, for they are grounded in God Himself. Though we may declare them invalid and outdated, they nevertheless retain their validity. Though we may contest their binding force on our lives, they remain binding for us. We shall be judged one day according to our works, that is, according to how far our actions measured up to the will of God made known to us in His commandments.

We may seek to evade this obligation by saying, 'But I believe in Jesus as my Saviour and have received forgiveness of my sins and therefore I shall stand justified before the judgment seat.' Even so, we are faced with the reality of the verse in Scripture, 'For we must all appear before the judgment seat of Christ; that every one may receive the things done in his body, according to that he hath done, whether it be good or bad' (2 Cor. 5:10 av).

It is the commandments of God that tell us what is good and bad. Many a believer has gone astray because he departed from the commandments of God (2 Pet. 2:20f.). Whoever turns aside from the commandments of God turns away from Jesus, the crucified Lord. For only when we recognise the validity of the commandments and acknowledge their claim upon us, can we come to the realisation of our sin. We shall see how often we fail and how unable we are to fulfil the commandments. And this in turn will lead us to contrition and repentance. Thus we are driven ever anew into the arms of Jesus Christ and to the foot of the cross. And in us grows a new, living relationship of faith to Jesus, our Saviour, who forgives us our sins and delivers us from the power of sin. We see then that there would be no recognition of sin and therefore no battle against sin if it were not for the commandments of God. Without the commandments we would not be aware of our sin and would not have any need of Jesus as our Saviour.

Here is the reason why so many believers are no longer spiritually alive, why they do not have a fervent love for Jesus, and as a result have no joy in Him, no love for lost souls nor love for their enemies; spiritually, some are just vegetating. Whoever does not take the commandments of God so seriously that he always tries to live according to them, whoever is not willing to capitulate before these standards and in sorrow and genuine contrition for his failings to believe in the merciful forgiveness of Jesus and trust in His grace will fall into spiritual death. Unfortunately, countless Christians rely on a cheap grace. That is, they do not wish their pardon to cost them anything. They want to receive it without striving to keep the commandments and without tears of contrition. The love that rejoices to know the will of God has grown cold in their hearts.

If the commandments lose their validity, the commission of Jesus Christ for the world also loses its validity. It was Jesus, the incarnate Word, the Commandment of God manifest in the flesh, who exemplified and proclaimed the one commandment that sums up all the others: the commandment of love. Without the commandments of God all law and order break down; the result is chaos. How true are the words that God spoke long ago after giving the commandments to His people! He declared, 'See, I have set before you this day life and good, death and evil' (Deut. 30:15). The choice is ours: If we acknowledge the commandments, we choose happiness; if we reject them, we choose unhappiness — for time and eternity.

This I have experienced in my own life in a very real way. During those years when I did not take the commandments of Jesus — to lose one's life, deny oneself, love one's enemies, etc. — as completely binding, I was not happy. I could sense that there was spiritual death in my life. But ever since I took God's commandments as absolutely obligatory, every failure to live up to them drove me into the arms of Jesus. As a result I became happy in Him. Spiritual life flowed into my heart and the Lord could use me anew in His service. It became clear to me that our fate for time and eternity depends upon our attitude towards the commandments, upon whether or not we strive to keep them.

Seeing that our life and happiness are determined by our attitude towards the commandments of God, we can never tire of holding them up before our eyes and inscribing them in our hearts as the standard for our lives.

But there is someone who begrudges us this life and happiness, and that is the Enemy. Using his subtle tactics, the Deceiver time and again seeks to bring our lives under a different standard, whispering in our ears: 'Did God really say', for instance, 'that I should not file a lawsuit, that my anger will bring the wrath of God down upon me, that I should not get a divorce, that the Bible calls every kind of marital relationship outside marriage, harlotry?' When we are assailed by such tempting voices, it is crucial that we listen to the voice of God, which comes to us with unmistakable clarity in the commandments written in His Word, and allow them to guide us in everyday life.

Whoever does not let the Enemy's voice penetrate his heart, but embraces God's commandments, daily taking a new commandment to heart and contemplating it (the 366 commandments in this book are meant as a help to this end), will discover something of the heart and nature of God. By acting upon God's commandments, he will become one with the will of God and thus with God Himself. God makes His dwelling with those who are one with His will, that is, with those who act according to His commandments; they are promised the deepest union with Him.

To take God's commandments seriously — what does this mean today? Apostasy and lawlessness are rampant, as Jesus had prophesied for the close of the age (Matt. 24:10ff.). As never before in the history of Christianity man can see with his own eyes that everyone who holds the commandments of God in contempt falls prey to

11

death. Today sin, drugs and venereal disease have imprinted the mark of death on millions. The suicide rate continues to rise. Violence, terrorism and murder are spreading. The heart of God is breaking for anguish. For did He not give the commandments for our well-being in body and soul? Yet man rejects them and rushes headlong into death and destruction. Misery is rampant. Human lives, families and entire nations are being destroyed.

Today, more than ever, it is unpardonable if we reject God's gracious offer contained in the commandments. Yes, in our times the consequences are exceedingly critical if we do not regard the commandments as binding. For we are not living in 'normal times'; the apocalyptic battle has commenced. On the one side is the 'lawless one', whose forerunners have already made their appearance and are dominating our times more and more. On the other side are those who keep God's commandments. Describing this battle, Scripture says, 'Then the dragon was angry with the woman, and went off to make war on the rest of her offspring, on those who keep the commandments of God' (Rev. 12:17). The consequences of whether or not we keep the commandments will be made manifest, for in this apocalyptic age everything becomes visible to the eye. If in previous ages a person did not regard the commandments as absolutely binding, he could still lead a respectable life. But today it is no longer possible to take a middle course. In the final battle, which has now begun between light and darkness, we are faced with an either/or situation.

The Enemy, knowing that his time is short, is determined to achieve his objective at all costs. He is determined to make us disregard the commandments of God. If we succumb, we come under his influence without realising it and eventually under his power. For whoever ceases to keep the commandments of God draws away from the dominion of God and enters the Enemy's domain. Accordingly, the decision that faces man nowadays is of far greater urgency than ever before in the past two thousand years. Either we choose to belong to God and His own, who keep His commandments, or we choose the lawless one, whose adherents dissolve the commandments of God. How terrible, therefore, is the present-day apostasy! Even in Christian circles the Ten Commandments are being discarded: for instance, premarital and extra-marital relations are condoned, the killing of unborn human life is accepted, and irreconciliation and slander are permitted to spread. In view of the blatant disregard for the commandments of God we should be gripped with a passionate desire to keep the commandments holy at all costs. In doing so, we prove that we love God, for Jesus says, 'If a man loves me, he will keep my word' (John 14:23). Conversely, this means that he who does not keep His commandments does not love God. He who despises them despises God. We do not realise how much guilt we heap upon ourselves when we say that we love Him but neglect to do His will, and this concerns also the 'minor' commandments. Strictly speaking, no commandment is minor, for Jesus regards them all as important. He says, 'Whoever then relaxes one of the least of these commandments and teaches men so, shall be called least in the kingdom of heaven' (Matt. 5:19). Let us, therefore, be willing to pay the price of obedience to God, for instance, by submitting to others in everyday life, or letting go of personal wishes and opinions, by overcoming fault-finding, bitterness, anger and envy, and practising selfless love. The price is so small when compared with the great treasure offered to us in His commandments, which are 'more precious than gold'.

May our everyday life, therefore, be a response to the tremendous offer of God, who as Love eternal has opened His heart and revealed to us something very precious and beautiful, imbued with everlasting life, glory and splendour — His commandments of love. Let us thank Him by demonstrating with our lives that the commandments can be kept in the power of our Lord Jesus Christ. And let us, by so doing, help to check the forces of evil active in our times, so that His kingdom of love may dawn in our midst.

In Praise of God's Commandments

Open my eyes, that I may behold wondrous things out of thy law. My soul is consumed with longing for thy ordinances at all times. Thy testimonies are my delight, they are my counsellors. I will run in the way of thy commandments.

Thou hast commanded thy precepts to be kept diligently. O that my ways may be steadfast in keeping thy statutes! I have laid up thy word in my heart, that I might not sin against thee.

With my lips I declare all the ordinances of thy mouth. I will meditate on thy precepts, and fix my eyes on thy ways. I will delight in thy statutes; I will not forget thy word.

Lead me in the path of thy commandments, for I delight in it. I will keep thy law continually, for ever and ever. I find my delight in thy commandments, which I love.

I revere thy commandments, which I love, and I will meditate on thy statutes. Thy statutes have been my songs in the house of my pilgrimage.

The Lord is my portion; I promise to keep thy words. I hasten and do not delay to keep thy commandments. The law of thy mouth is better to me than thousands of gold and silver pieces. Thy law is my delight. All thy commandments are sure. I will never forget thy precepts; for by them thou hast given me life.

Oh, how I love thy law! It is my meditation all the day. How sweet are thy words to my taste, sweeter than honey to my mouth! Thy word is a lamp to my feet and a light to my path.

Thy testimonies are my heritage for ever; yea, they are the joy of my heart. Therefore I love thy commandments above gold, above fine gold. I direct my steps by all thy precepts. Thy testimonies are wonderful; therefore my soul keeps them.

Thy commandments are my delight. I love thy precepts! The sum of thy word is truth; and every one of thy righteous ordinances endures for ever.

I rejoice at thy word like one who finds great spoil. I praise thee for thy righteous ordinances. Great peace have those who love thy law. My soul keeps thy testimonies; I love them exceedingly.

My tongue will sing of thy word, for all thy commandments are right. Thy law is my delight.

taken from Psalm 119

Prayer

Our Lord Jesus Christ,

You are the Commandment of love, incarnate and manifest, having lived it out in obedience day by day, even unto death upon the cross. For this we thank You.

Jesus, You are our only hope in view of the holy demands God makes in His commandments and our inability to fulfil them, for You live in us and it is You who fulfil them in us if we believe in You and live in close communion with You, bound to You as the branches are to the vine.

We thank You that it is true that Your commandments are not difficult for us to fulfil, because we can claim Your sacrifice and reckon with Your victory. Our Lord Jesus Christ, You desire to be mighty in us, and with Your help we can do all things; thus we can also keep Your commandments. We worship You, because You are more powerful than our egoistic and sinful nature.

We thank You that through Your death and resurrection You have set Your seal upon the truth that God's commandments can be fulfilled. You have not only called us, but redeemed us. We believe in Your redemption, and in our hearts we yearn for the fulfilment of Your great promise that You will make Your home with those who keep Your word.

Amen.

January

The commandments of God
are not tablets of prohibitions,
but signposts that point the way
to life and joy.

1

Be not afraid, only believe. Mark 5:36b AV

Believe in the victory and promises of Jesus. Reckon with them. Praise His victory daily over all the impossible situations in your personal life and in your work for the Kingdom of God, and you will behold His victory and the glory of God both here and above. God reveals Himself to the eyes of faith.

2

Sing to the Lord, bless his name; tell of his salvation from day to day. Ps. 96:2

Sing your praises to God every day, especially when you are not in the mood, when you are weighed down by burdens within and without. By singing and praising His name, you will call down His help. You will experience that God inclines Himself to you and fills your life with His spirit of peace and joy and comfort.

3

My children, let us love not merely in theory or in words — let us love in sincerity and in practice! 1 John 3:18 JBP

If you wish to love others in sincerity and practice, take the grain of wheat as your example. It falls into the ground and dies. The love of Jesus was victorious, because He laid down His life for others. Likewise, for you too there is only one way to walk in true love — and that is, to die to self, to your rights and claims in daily life and in your relationship with your neighbour. Only if you do so, will your words of love be genuine and capable of reaching the hearts of others.

4

Take no part in the unfruitful works of darkness, but instead expose them.　　　　　Eph. 5:11

Do you seek the approval of God or of men? Whoever wishes to please God must be ready to lose the favour of men when it means saying a true word to rebuke and expose the works of darkness. The Lord expects His own to speak such words. He expects them to speak out, for instance, against the mockery of that which is holy, divine or good, because this is His commandment. Only those who obey the commandments of God will have His blessing on their lives, actions and service for Him.

5

Cease from anger and forsake wrath; fret not yourself; it tends only to evil-doing.　　Ps. 37:8 AB

Anger is a bitter root that poisons our heart. This poison often flows from us invisibly, unknown to ourselves. However, it causes great damage to the soul of our neighbour and brings down the wrath of God upon us, for we have sinned against him. Therefore, do not tolerate any reproachful or bitter thought against others in your heart. Refusal to forgive others will close the door of God's heart to you.

6

Live in such a way that no one will ever be offended or kept back from finding the Lord by the way we act. 2 Cor. 6:3 LB

God wishes to gather into His household all His children who are still standing outside. Do not repel them by your conduct and thus bar their way into the Father's house. If you do, they will bear witness against you at the Last Judgment. Rather, live up to your calling, so that your example will draw many to God and inspire them to follow Jesus. It should be obvious to all from your life that following Jesus makes a person rich in love, and therefore cheerful and happy.

7

Wake up! Strengthen what little remains — for even what is left is at the point of death.
Rev. 3:2a LB

Even if you are aware of no sin other than lukewarmness and sleepiness in your spiritual life, do not forget that they are the hotbed for all other sins. When a person is asleep, he sees nothing. In the spiritual sense this means he is blind to his sin. He does not battle against it and therefore he cannot overcome. He will lose all that he has gained in the way of spiritual life, and being dead himself, he is incapable of rousing others to life. So say to Jesus, the Prince of life, 'Rouse me by Your life-giving Spirit!' Do not cease to pray this in faith, so that you will not only be saved from eternal death, but be able to lead others to new life.

8

Keep your steps from wavering.　　Heb. 12:13 NEB

Walk the path of uncompromising discipleship. Then your steps will not waver. You will be following a way that has already been paved, for Jesus has trodden it before you — a path that leads directly to the goal. Therefore, whenever you are unsure what your path and your course of action should be, choose the path that Jesus trod before you — the path of lowliness, humility, forgiveness and love. And your path, like His, will end in glory.

9

Persevere in prayer.　　Col. 4:2 NEB

Only those who pray with implicit faith in the victory of Jesus can persevere in prayer. When you pray, call to mind ever anew Jesus' victory of the resurrection. Praise His victory. Claim it. And in the end the Enemy will be forced to yield. The name of Jesus always brings victory and breaks the power of Satan. This will be the sure experience of those who do not grow tired of persevering in prayer and praising His victory until they see the fulfilment.

10

Never flag in zeal, be aglow with the Spirit, serve the Lord.   Rom. 12:11

Only a burning zeal can impart ardour and set others aflame. So do not tolerate any lukewarmness in your spiritual life. The Lord will spew the lukewarm out of His mouth. They cause more harm to the establishment of the Kingdom of God than those who are cold. So pray earnestly for the Spirit of divine ardour, who is promised to those who ask for Him. Claim this promise in faith and He will come into your heart and equip you to serve God mightily.

11

Draw nigh to God, and he will draw nigh to you. Cleanse your hands, ye sinners; and purify your hearts, ye double minded.   Jas. 4:8 AV

Remember that when your soul draws near to God, He will draw near to you. Therefore, take

25

every opportunity to come apart and draw close to God in prayer. And God will incline Himself to you — provided that you first let your heart and hands be cleansed. If there is any sin you are aware of, confess it before God and your fellow men and break with it, so that there will be no barrier between you and God.

12

Is any one among you suffering? Let him pray.

Jas. 5:13

We generally do just the opposite. We stop praying when our hearts are sorrowful. This is the Enemy's objective. He knows that prayer is our sole help in extreme distress. Only prayer can transform our sad hearts and the whole distressing situation in and about us. Therefore, do not listen to the voice of the Enemy when you are in suffering. Rather, listen to the voice of God. Heed His challenge. Even though you may not feel like it, start to pray — and prayer will help you. Indeed, you will receive a special blessing as a result of your suffering, for it will drive you to pray more and bring you into deeper communion with God — the greatest joy of all.

13

Hearken, O daughter, and consider, and incline thine ear; forget also thine own people, and thy father's house; So shall the king greatly desire thy beauty: for he is thy Lord; and worship thou him.
Ps. 45:10f. AV

God's approval rests upon those, who, for His sake, leave all else behind, yes, count all things as naught, in order to win Christ. So out of love for Him give up that which you hold dear, and you will receive the most precious gift of all — God Himself.

14

No bad language must pass your lips, but only what is good and helpful to the occasion, so that it brings a blessing to those who hear it.
Eph. 4:29 NEB

It is no trifling matter to indulge in evil, indecent or frivolous talk, or even to listen to it. Jesus says, 'If you are a cause of stumbling to one of these little ones who have faith in Me' — and how easily this can occur through such talk — 'it would be better for you to have a millstone hung round your neck.' So take care that everything you say or do can serve to be a blessing for others.

15

Preach the Word of God urgently at all times, whenever you get the chance, in season and out, when it is convenient and when it is not.

2 Tim. 4:2 LB

The power of your ministry stems from the insults and humiliations your service earns you for Jesus' sake. Therefore, only be concerned with God's task for you and His commands, and never with human opinions. Pay no heed to rebuffs and abuse, but rather bear testimony to God's Word and His will, and your labours will yield great fruit.

16

Let not your hearts be troubled; believe in God, believe also in me.
John 14:1

Nothing can be greater than Jesus — not even your sins, your disposition, your troubles. He is greater than everything. Believe this, even if you seem to experience nothing but failures and disappointments. Then the greatest hardships and battles of faith will end in victory.

17

Do your best to win full approval in God's sight, as a worker who is not ashamed of his work.

2 Tim. 2:15 GNB

It is worth doing our best for God to show ourselves as labourers approved by Him, for then, according to Jesus' promise, we shall one day be received by Him at the gate of eternity with the words, 'Well done, good and faithful servant . . . Enter into the joy of your master.' To receive such a verdict for eternity, it is surely but a small thing to give ourselves completely and do our utmost for the Kingdom of God.

18

Go, sell what you possess and give to the poor, and you will have treasure in heaven; and come, follow me.   Matt. 19:21

Not just once but ever anew give of your earthly treasures, be they material goods or privileges and honours. Then you will have treasure in heaven. Indeed, the more closely you follow in Jesus' footsteps here below on the path of poverty and self-denial out of love, the nearer you will be to Him, the King of heaven, one day above.

JANUARY

19

Let all things be done decently and in order.

1 Cor. 14:40 AV

God is a God of order. He detests all that is disorderly and indecent. If you want Jesus to dwell in your home, in your family, at your place of work, make sure that order and discipline reign there. Start by clearing your heart and life of all ulterior motives, of all that is disorderly or impure. Then Jesus will delight to dwell in your heart and home.

20

When you pray, go into your room and shut the door and pray to your Father who is in secret; and your Father who sees in secret will reward you.

Matt. 6:6

God, who is holy and eternal, is also the essence of love, and He does not wish to remain alone. He is seeking your soul. He wishes to converse with you, to reveal Himself to you. But He speaks only when all within and about you is silent. Therefore, seek silence and solitude ever anew, and they will bring you the greatest of all gifts — communion with the living God. (See also *Praying Our Way through Life*)

21

*Ye should shew forth the praises of him who hath
called you out of darkness into his marvellous
light.* 1 Pet. 2:9b AV

God has called you to bear witness to Him, the
Lord, who is the Light of the world. But you will
only be a light to the world, illumining the way
for others, in so far as you banish all sin and
secretiveness from your heart and life. Only if
you are willing to bring your hidden sins into the
light, can you testify to the victory of Jesus ever
anew and pave the way for His kingdom of light.

22

*Agree among yourselves, and avoid divisions; be
firmly joined in unity of mind and thought.*
1 Cor. 1:10 NEB

Disciples of Jesus are called to practise and
demonstrate the unity of love with each other. So
never be at variance with anyone, even if it is
merely by erecting a barrier in your heart against
a fellow believer. God is warning you. If you allow
the spirit of discord room in your life, you will
soon no longer have a part in the kingdom of
Jesus, which is a kingdom of love, and above you
will not be present at the wedding feast of His
bridal host, whose characteristic feature is love.

23

When you give alms, do not let your left hand know what your right hand is doing, so that your alms may be in secret. Matt. 6:3f.

When you have done a good deed, ask the Lord to erase it from your memory. Do not speak about it or even think about it. Do not be pleased with yourself. Instead, resist such thoughts and all desire for recognition. And in heaven the Lord will reward you openly for the good that you have done.

24

Let there be no more resentment, no more anger or temper, no more violent self-assertiveness, no more slander and no more malicious remarks.
Eph. 4:31 JBP

If Jesus is Lord in your life, then peace, forgiveness and gentleness reign. Whoever gives resentment, anger, violent self-assertiveness and slander the right to rule in his heart or home drives away Jesus, who is the Prince of Peace. Jesus does not share a dwelling with such fellow lodgers. If they threaten to poison your life, even in the slightest degree, part with them this very day.

25

Be ready at any time to give a quiet and reverent answer to any man who wants a reason for the hope that you have within you. 1 Pet. 3:15 JBP

An incomparable hope has been granted to us. In heaven Jesus is waiting for us in great love. He has prepared joy and ineffable glory for us for all eternity. Live in the thought of the joys that await you. This will spur you on to tell others about the hope that is in you. Joy will radiate from you and shine into a world filled with hopelessness, for joy is contagious.

26

You must have nothing to do with any so-called Christian who leads a loose life, or is grasping, or idolatrous, a slanderer, a drunkard, or a swindler. You should not even eat with any such person.
1 Cor. 5:11 NEB

God is calling you to sever connections with evildoers. If you cover up another's sin by not taking a stand against it, you involve yourself. Not only do you share the guilt of his sin, but you encourage him in his sinning. Whoever fears God, who judges and punishes sin, instead of fearing his brother, will have the courage to break with his erring brother who persists in sin. Whom do you fear?

JANUARY

27

Above all these put on love, which binds everything together in perfect harmony.   Col. 3:14

Disciples of Jesus are called to be peacemakers of His kingdom of love. Jesus bids them to do everything in their power to establish unity where there is discord. So never look on with indifference when you encounter dissension in the Body of Christ. Seek to heal the breach by walking in humble love. Yes, be willing to step into the breach, even if it means dying to self. And believe that when we offer ourselves up for the sake of others and are willing to be given the blame, to be scorned and ostracised, we pave the way for the love of Jesus to be victorious and to bind everything together in perfect harmony.

28

Wait for the Lord; be strong, take courage, and wait for the Lord.   Ps. 27:14 NEB

Be patient and learn to wait humbly for God's moment. His aid will always come, even if it seems to tarry. His timing is always perfect. Believe that because He loves you, He will never send His aid too late. Indeed, even now as you wait in patience, you will experience His aid, for He will strengthen you and carry you through. Impatience, discouragement and lack of faith, on the other hand, hinder Him from coming to help.

29

You must be self-controlled and alert, to be able to pray.   1 Pet. 4:7 GNB

If you want your prayers to reach the throne of God and be answered, fulfil the necessary prerequisite. Lead a life of self-control. Be disciplined in your words and actions, in eating, drinking and sleeping, and with regard to sensual pleasure. By ever anew placing all areas of your life under the dominion of Jesus Christ, remove the obstacles that prevent your prayers from being answered. Then you will always experience the help and grace of God in your life.

30

Humble yourselves before the Lord, and he will lift you up.   Jas. 4:10 GNB

Let no opportunity pass by to break your pride. Humble yourself before God and men whenever the Spirit of God moves you to do so. Do not heed the pain it will bring you, for the fruit is incomparable. God grants grace to the humble, yes, He lifts them up to His throne and takes them to His heart.

JANUARY

31

The Lord's servant must not quarrel. He must be kind towards all.   2 Tim. 2:24 GNB

Quarrelling and strife come from hell. They create hell on earth for people in any fellowship, home or place of work; and whoever persists in these sins will be barred from the Kingdom of God in the next world. Therefore, more than anything else, avoid quarrelsomeness if you want to be a true servant of Jesus and not a servant of evil. Make it your aim to reflect the image of your Lord, who is the essence of gentleness and kindness.

February

How amazing and awe-inspiring it
is that the eternal and most high
God should reveal Himself to us
men, that He should speak and
proclaim what we are to do and
what will serve to our good!
Must not His heart, therefore, be
deeply wounded when we disregard
His words and commandments?

1

Obey your leaders and submit to them.

Heb. 13:17

If you want to bring a sacrifice of love, obedience is the greatest sacrifice you can make. For it entails letting yourself be broken and even your most devout desires and wishes frustrated. Because this hurts and costs you something, it is a genuine sacrifice, which will give you authority in your service for the Lord. Power and blessing are granted only to those who are obedient to God and their superiors, unless, of course, the latter demand something that is against the will of God.

2

Rejoice in your hope. Rom. 12:12

Live in the future glory that is prepared for you; rejoice in the hope of that which awaits you above. Then the coming glory and all its joy will become a present-day reality for you. Live in this hope, and the sadness within you and about you will disappear.

3

Avoid stupid controversies, genealogies, dissensions, and quarrels over the law, for they are unprofitable and futile. Titus 3:9

Whatever is not born of love is worthless in the eyes of God. And this also goes for religious controversies and legalistic arguments in which we egoistically insist that our opinion is right. Avoid them, for such dissensions spell death to your spiritual life and the spiritual life in the Church of God.

4

If any one forces you to go one mile, go with him two miles. Matt. 5:41

Do not merely fulfil the request made of you. Always do more than people ask of you — even when it costs you much. Then your heavenly Father will bestow upon you a double portion of His goodness.

5

Covetousness must not even be named among you. Eph. 5:3

Whoever craves for money, wealth and a higher standard of living will find that this craving will ruin his spiritual life. Jesus became poor for our sakes, so that by His poverty we might become rich. Be of the same mind as He and you will receive spiritual riches and happiness. Yes, you will even be able to enrich the lives of many others with that which you receive from God in your poverty.

6

A man of understanding holds his peace.

Prov. 11:12 NEB

If you wish to follow Jesus, the Lamb of God, remain silent when you come under attack. There is power in keeping silent. But do not remain silent because your feelings are hurt or because you have given up hope for the others. Instead, bless the others in humble love, and ask forgiveness for whenever you may have sinned against them, perhaps by simply not loving them enough. Such humble love will far more readily win others over than anything else.

7

Strengthen the weak hands, and make firm the feeble knees. Say to those who are of a fearful heart, 'Be strong, fear not! Behold, your God will come.'

Isa. 35:3f.

Keep your eyes open and see if anyone about you is sad and discouraged. God has charged you with the commission to encourage the downhearted with a word of comfort, with a verse of Scripture or a piece of literature that you could pass on to

41

them. Do not miss the opportunity to pull someone out of his despair. Otherwise, he could testify against you one day in eternity.

8

Cease to do evil, learn to do good; seek justice.
Isa. 1:16f.

If you do not know how to be victorious over the evil within you, pray for hatred against it. Hatred has power to kill. The more you hate your sin, the more you will love goodness. Love contains tremendous power. By loving goodness, you will be able to practise it in the power of Jesus' redemption.

9

Therefore be imitators of God, as beloved children. And walk in love.
Eph. 5:1f.

The love of God is without limit and without end. He bids us to follow His example. Therefore, never give a person up. Never say you are finished with him, no matter how much harm he may have done to you. Only if you continue to love your neighbour in patience, can you be sure of God's patient love for yourself.

10

Remember the sabbath day, to keep it holy.

Exod. 20:8

We often give generously of our time to be with loved ones. They are worth so much to us. God too is asking for our time. He is asking us to give Him one day in the week in addition to our daily prayer time. In His love He yearns to have communion with us in a special way. On this day in particular He wants to speak with us like a father with his children. He longs to hear our voice and response in prayer, to receive tokens of our love as we sing to Him and rejoice in thanksgiving for all the good gifts that He has bestowed upon us. What a grief it must be for Him when He waits in vain for us on this day! Do you set apart this one day, Sunday, for Him as the Lord's day?

11

Seek ye first the kingdom of God, and his righteousness; and all these things shall be added unto you. Matt. 6:33 AV

Whoever truly spends himself for the coming of the Kingdom of God cannot do otherwise than look to his heavenly Father in childlike trust for all his needs. He lives for God and so he relies on Him and His help. Therefore, trust the Father implicitly in every situation, in hardship and peril. He will never disappoint you. Rather, He will shower you with all His goodness if you live wholly for Jesus and His kingdom.

12

Rid yourselves, then, of all evil; no more lying or hypocrisy or jealousy or insulting language.

1 Pet. 2:1 GNB

Flee envy and hypocrisy at the very onset, for it was envy and slander that were responsible for Jesus' death on the cross. If you love Him, you will not crucify Him anew with such evil-mindedness.

13

Lead a life worthy of the calling to which you have been called, with all lowliness and meekness, with patience, forbearing one another in love.

Eph. 4:1f.

You are called to bring Christ to others, to reflect the image of Jesus — the image of lowliness, meekness and patience. Remember that you bring discredit to your Lord and Saviour in the sight of the world when you do not walk worthy of your calling.

14

Do not be overcome by evil, but overcome evil with good. Rom. 12:21

How can you withstand evil? There is a way — the way of lowliness. The humble are too lowly for the arrows of the Evil One to strike them. Since the Enemy, from whom all evil comes, never gets down on his knees, as the humble do, the arrows fly high above their heads. So maintain a humble attitude towards him who does you wrong, and you will be victorious in humble love.

15

Show yourself in all respects a model of good deeds. Titus 2:7

God rejoices in good deeds, for, as Jesus says, the heavenly Father will be given glory for them. Does God find works of love, works of meekness, works of patience in your life? He has a right to expect them, for His only-begotten Son has redeemed you to perform such works. Remember that if your faith is genuine, it will bring forth the fruit of good works. Faith without works is dead.

16

Make love your aim. 1 Cor. 14:1

Let love be your highest aim. Pursue it more than any other gift. Desire to be richer in love than in

FEBRUARY

anything else, for nothing in heaven or on earth is as precious as love. Discard all self-love as you would rubbish. And make room in your heart for His love — a love that loves its neighbour as itself.

17

Apply thine heart unto instruction, and thine ears to the words of knowledge.   Prov. 23:12 AV

Every act of obedience to the will of God begins by listening to what He has to say to us in His Word or through people. Listen to the advice, warnings and reproaches that you receive and take them to heart. Otherwise, you will miss out on priceless riches for your spiritual life.

18

Take care, brethren, lest there be in any of you an evil, unbelieving heart, leading you to fall away from the living God.   Heb. 3:12

An unbelieving heart is declared by God to be evil. Why? Because it mistrusts God, and mistrust is evil — it gnaws at your soul and grieves the heart of God. Indeed, mistrust and unbelief separate you from the living God. One thing, however, can help you to overcome unbelief and mistrust. Picture to yourself the image of Jesus, the Lamb of God, in His amazing love for you. Worship the Father for His unending love in giving His only-begotten Son as a sacrifice for you. Then you will not be able to do otherwise than trust Him.

19

Tell them not to speak evil of anyone. Titus 3:2 GNB

If you speak sarcastically about others — perhaps without even realising that you are slandering them — you may very quickly find yourself on the side of Jesus' enemies, for they tried to make Him look ridiculous and ended up by blaspheming Him. Then you too will be counted among His enemies. Therefore, let no disparaging remarks or slander pass your lips, and do not tolerate such talk in your presence, so that the Lord will not pronounce the verdict one day, 'Away with him! I do not know him!'

20

Those who live should no longer live for them-selves, but only for him who died and was raised to life for their sake. 2 Cor. 5:15 GNB

Do not dwell on any self-centred thoughts, on thoughts of self-pity or self-assertion. Bring such thoughts to Jesus; centre your attention on Him — and He will lift you out of all self-centredness. Yes, He will fill your life with His presence and enrich it.

21

Buy the truth and sell it not. Prov. 23:23 AV

Whenever we buy something, there is a price to pay. Has it already cost you something to honour the truth by bringing a falsehood or lie into the light and confessing it? Truth is something precious. If we live in the truth, speak the truth, accept the truth, we belong to Jesus, the King of truth. But liars and all those who love falsehood will one day stand outside the City of God according to Holy Scripture (Rev. 22:15). So make your choice!

22

Avoid the profane talk and foolish arguments of what some people wrongly call 'Knowledge'.
1 Tim. 6:20 GNB

Do not get involved in any arguments or indulge in empty chatter. Rather, speak first with God; bring everything that is on your heart to Him in prayer. Then you will not egoistically insist that your opinions about spiritual matters are right and you will not be at odds with other believers. Instead your words will be a spirit-filled testimony of life and love. They will lead others to Jesus or build up their faith and bring you fruit.

23

He who humbles himself will be exalted.

Luke 18:14

When people criticise you justly, respond like the publican, humbling yourself beneath your sin, 'God, be merciful to me, a sinner.' For God gives grace to the humble and you will go forth justified, absolved from sin and declared righteous by God for time and eternity.

24

Spare no effort to make fast with bonds of peace the unity which the Spirit gives. Eph. 4:3 NEB

Are you at odds with anyone? The instructions of the Lord are thus: spare no effort to re-tie the bond of peace. What have you done to this end? What price have you paid to maintain unity or to be reconciled when there was division? A broken bond with a fellow man can result in a broken bond between you and God.

25

Come, let us bow down and worship him.

Ps. 95:6 GNB

God is waiting for worshippers who cast themselves down at His feet in spirit and bring honour, glory and praise to the Father, the Lamb and the Holy Spirit. Lift up your voices. Let your homes and churches be ever filled with the strains of praise. When God is worshipped, heaven comes down, for worship and heaven belong together. So bow down in worship, and praise the goodness of the heavenly Father, the mercy of the Lamb of God and the love of the Holy Spirit. Then heaven will come down to you too.

26

Put off your old nature which belongs to your former manner of life and is corrupt through deceitful lusts. Eph. 4:22

It was a sinful desire that caused the first human beings to fall to such depths. And to this day craving has been one of the characteristics of our old self. The devil takes advantage of this situation and tries to make us become addicted to his poison, so that we shall meet our downfall inwardly and outwardly. Therefore, be resolute. Whenever your old self makes himself noticeable in your heart with his deceitful desires, renounce him in faith in Jesus' redemption, so that you do not fall under Satan's power. Then you will experience that whenever you lose your life for Jesus' sake, that is, whenever you put the old self to death together with all that seems so desirable to you, you will gain true, eternal riches, real joy and complete satisfaction.

27

*Remember the wonderful works that he has done,
his miracles, and the judgments he uttered.*

Ps. 105:5

Never forget to call to mind all the miracles, great
and small, that God has performed for you and
continues to perform even in the smallest details
of your life. This will strengthen your faith and
give you courage. You will become bold, and in
the face of new difficulties and seemingly impossible situations, you will be able to declare trium-
phantly, 'We have a God who performs miracles!'
And this faith will let you experience new miracles of God.

28

*Your conduct among the heathen should be so
good that when they accuse you of being evildoers,
they will have to recognise your good deeds and
so praise God on the Day of his coming.*

1 Pet. 2:12 GNB

The Word of God forbids us to take people to
court in order to avenge ourselves when they
slander us. It shows us another way to win over
our adversaries — and that is to walk in love as
Jesus did. Love is forgiving; it does good to its
enemies and is ready to be reconciled. Our behaviour will be far more convincing than all our talk-
ing and God will be given glory for our conduct.
So choose this way, and God will contend for you.

FEBRUARY

29

Acknowledge those who are working so hard among you, and in the Lord's fellowship are your leaders and counsellors. Hold them in the highest possible esteem and affection for the work they do. 1 Thess. 5:12f. NEB

If you are humble, you will appreciate what others do for you, especially if they have helped you to find the right path again when you have gone astray. This will kindle you with love and gratitude. What have you done to show your love and thanks to your spiritual counsellors? God is waiting for you to demonstrate your appreciation.

March

The commandments of God,
which spring from His loving heart,
are a challenge for us to love God
and our fellow men.
Whoever practises this love
fulfils the entire Law,
for all the commandments
are based on love.

1

Let us keep our eyes fixed on Jesus, on whom our faith depends from beginning to end. Heb. 12:2 GNB

Do not let your thoughts be filled with your self, for behind your self is the Enemy, who is waiting to ensnare you. Rather let your thoughts be filled with Jesus, His redemption and His victory. Look to Him in faith — and He will lift you out of the depths of despair and take you to His heart.

2

Follow in his steps . . . When he was reviled, he did not revile in return . . . but he trusted to him who judges justly. 1 Pet. 2:21,23

Follow in Jesus' footsteps along the path of the Lamb, and when you are slandered and reviled, do not revile in return. Rather, in your heart, bless those who heap disgrace upon you. And in His time God will vindicate you. Indeed, you will discover that this way, which is so foolish in the eyes of the world, is the wisest way of all.

3

If we have food and clothes, that should be enough for us. But those who want to get rich fall into temptation. 1 Tim. 6:8f. GNB

Before making a new purchase that is not absolutely necessary, ask yourself whether it is greed and thus the Devil that is prompting you. The Enemy has nothing good in mind for you. So be careful. Do not fall into his snare; protect yourself by giving thanks ever anew for everything that God in His goodness has granted you for your daily life. And learn to be content with that which you have.

4

Honour your father and your mother.   Exod. 20:12

God bids us to honour our parents, for He knows that with our fault-finding, bitterness and pride, we often sin against them. God has not appointed us to pass judgment over our parents. That is His concern. Consequently, we are infringing upon God's rights when we act as judges over our parents. Our responsibility towards them is of a different nature. We are to honour them as people who have been created in the image of God, although the image they bear may be distorted and sinful. If we honour a person, we respect his will and wishes, give him gifts and are of service to him. Is this how we act towards our parents?

5

Love endures all things.   1 Cor. 13:7

Jesus endured all things for us, so open wide your heart and let Him give you His love. Then your heart will brim over with forgiving love for your neighbour, even when he wrongs you time and again. And if you show such forgiving love towards your neighbour, God will bathe you in the rivers of His mercy.

6

Exhort yourselves.　　　　　1 Thess. 5:11 AV (note)

Exhort your soul by saying, 'Rise and pray!' 'Take this opportunity to sow love.' 'Here is a chance to deny yourself.' 'Steer clear of this sin!' Such exhortation has power. It makes you begin to call upon the Lord, because you can sense your inability to live up to such challenges, and this realisation will drive you into the arms of Jesus, who wants to help you to fulfil them.

7

He that would love life and see good days, let him keep his tongue from evil and his lips from speaking guile.　　　　　1 Pet. 3:10

Many of the woes and ills in your life are your own doing. There is a connection between the difficult relationships, discord and divisions you complain about and the sins of your tongue. Instead of quarrelling with others, be silent and in prayer let God convict you of your sinful words and actions. Pray for your neighbour who makes life difficult for you, bless him and speak well of him. Then your life will be freed of gloom and bitterness, and it will be characterised by peace and joy instead.

8

O that you had hearkened to my commandments! Then your peace would have been like a river, and your righteousness like the waves of the sea.
Isa. 48:18

Keep the covenant holy that the Lord your God has made with you in Jesus, by keeping His commandments holy, regarding them as binding and acting according to them. For great is the curse and punishment incurred by those who break the holiest of covenants and disregard His commandments — just as the stream of divine peace and blessing is great that is poured over those who keep His commandments.

9

Do not spread false rumours.　　　Exod. 23:1 GNB

To repeat unfavourable reports about someone else without checking their verity can amount to slander. In this way you could become guilty of destroying the good reputation of your neighbour. However, this is a violation of the sixth commandment, and offenders, as Jesus says, are 'liable to the hell of fire' (Matt. 5:22). So before making statements about your neighbour, examine them in the sight of God.

10

Give, and it will be given to you; good measure, pressed down, shaken together, running over, will be put into your lap.   Luke 6:38

Give when people ask of you, but especially when God asks of you. Never tire of giving. Give away the things your heart clings to. And God will bestow upon you the fullness of grace and love, which are His to grant.

11

Let us therefore strive to enter that rest. Heb. 4:11

Who will one day enter the eternal rest of our home above in the kingdom of light? Only he who allowed himself no rest until he had attained this goal and who, therefore, was set on having his heart cleansed of the dust of everyday life and being sanctified. Are you gripped by the same fervour to pursue this goal? Whoever enters a race puts forth every effort to gain the trophy. How much have we already done to reach this eternal goal?

MARCH

12

I appeal to you therefore, brethren, by the mercies of God, to present your bodies as a living sacrifice, holy and acceptable to God, which is your spiritual worship. Rom. 12:1

In sacrificing we find true life. The more your life is marked by sacrifices, the more fruit it will bring you for all eternity. Therefore, let no opportunity to sacrifice slip by, especially when it is a chance for you to present your body — its desires or its well-being — as a sacrifice. But never do so as an act of asceticism. Rather, let it always be a genuine sacrifice in loving response to the mercies of God.

13

Do not grieve the Holy Spirit of God, in whom you were sealed for the day of redemption. Eph. 4:30

The Holy Spirit leads and guides us with unending love; day by day He works to transform us. He wants to be our Comforter and Helper. So take this command of Scripture very seriously and heed the gentle admonitions of the Spirit, so that you do not drive Him out of your heart and life. A life without His guidance and admonition is an empty one; it often runs along the wrong track and does not end in the Kingdom of God.

14

Call upon me in the day of trouble; I will deliver you, and you shall glorify me.   Ps. 50:15

When you are sitting in the depths of your fear, distress and temptation, raise your head and look up. God is not to be found in the depths of your misery, but rather outside of you — above, in the heights of His sanctuary. He is waiting for you to look up to Him and cry for help. So call upon Him and you will experience His help.

15

Make no provision for the flesh, to gratify its desires.   Rom. 13:14

Your body was given to you by God, so that you may glorify Him with it. But the desires of the flesh war against the spirit. Proclaim the victory of Jesus in prayer, so that your sinful desires will not get the better of you. Your eternal destiny is at stake, for your wicked deeds will follow you into eternity and accuse you on the day of judgment.

16

Take no part in the sins of others.   1 Tim. 5:22 GNB

Whoever glosses over the sins of another will also be held responsible for these sins. Only if you bring them into the light and take no part in them, will you be spared the judgment that will fall upon the other person, for you have warned him earnestly. So for your own sake and the sake of your neighbour be on your guard against not calling sin sin, even if others try to mislead you with arguments about so-called brotherly love.

17

Exhort servants to be obedient unto their own masters.　　　　　　　　　　　Titus 2:9 AV

Someone has to give the orders and bear the weight of responsibility. And someone has to serve and submit himself. Otherwise it would not be possible for there to be peace, harmony and order among people on earth. As a disciple of Jesus you are called to serve, for Jesus said, 'I am among you as one who serves.' So whenever God puts you in a position where you are required to submit, do so in voluntary love and dedication to Jesus. In this way you will prove your strength, for the strength to serve is far greater than the strength to rule. This is what made Jesus so majestic. Then you will reign with Him in truth, being freed from pride, selfish ambition and thirst for power, which so easily enslave us.

18

Set your minds on things that are above, not on things that are on earth. Col. 3:2

Do not seek earthly, transient things; do not worry about them. Such worries bind you to this earth. Trust and reckon with the might of your Father, who is in heaven. Then not only will you experience His power, but your heart will be bound to heaven and you will bring heaven down.

19

Hold fast what you have, so that no one may seize your crown. Rev. 3:11

In the storms of temptation and amid the onslaughts of the Enemy's forces, cling firmly to the instructions in the Word of God and follow them exactly. Proclaim the victorious name of Jesus time and again over your temptations and you will be able to remain faithful. By acting in obedience and faith, you will reach the goal and receive the glorious crown of victory at the end of your life.

MARCH

20

Share your food with the hungry and open your homes to the homeless poor. Give clothes to those who have nothing to wear, and do not refuse to help your own relatives. Isa. 58:7 GNB

Keep an open eye for the needs about you. Remember the poor, the hungry, the lonely and the needy and do good to them. Do not follow the natural inclinations of your heart and merely care for your nearest and dearest. Whatever goodness you show to the needy is regarded as an act of love by the Lord, and He will reward you at the resurrection of the righteous.

21

Let us conduct ourselves becomingly as in the day, not in revelling and drunkenness, not in debauchery and licentiousness. Rom. 13:13

We must all appear before the judgment seat of Christ one day (2 Cor. 5:10). If you sin by indulging in sensualism or sexual immorality, you stand under the judgment of God and will — according to Scripture — forfeit the Kingdom of God. Therefore, beware of immoderation and lack of discipline with regard to the gratification of desires. Avoid them more than anything else. Battle against them in faith in the redeeming power of the blood of Jesus Christ.

22

Ask, and it will be given you.   Matt. 7:7a

He who asks not receives not. He who asks for little receives little. He who asks for much receives much. So ask much of your Father in heaven and you will receive abundantly and will have much reason to praise and honour Him.

23

Behold, happy is the man whom God reproves; therefore despise not the chastening of the Almighty.   Job 5:17

Part of God's nature as a true and loving Father is to raise and discipline His children. In His love God uses blows of chastening in order to pull individuals and nations out of the quicksands of sin, which would be their ruin. He wants to bring about repentance and deliverance. Therefore, do not resist the chastenings of God, for they are actually an offer of tremendous grace. Accept them willingly and humbly and you will experience help and healing for your life on earth and attain great glory in eternity.

65

MARCH

24

Build up your strength in union with the Lord and by means of his mighty power.   Eph. 6:10 GNB

You need no longer be afraid whenever you feel weak and powerless, for you can enjoy the fullness of strength in your weakness. Live in close communion with Jesus, and God's strength will flow into you — just as the invigorating sap of the vine flows into its branches. So take care today to keep intact this union with the Lord, who is the source of your strength.

25

Freely ye have received, freely give.   Matt. 10:8 AV

When God has given you something — spiritual or material — respond with thanks. And as you rejoice over His goodness, show your gratitude by being kind to others and giving them gifts with a cheerful heart. In this way you will bring joy to God's heart.

26

He who hates his life in this world will keep it for eternal life.   John 12:25b

Hate your ego with all its demands for attention, love and honour. And hatred will kill it, making room for love towards God and man. Then, by practising genuine love, you will taste paradise on earth and inherit eternal life above.

27

Let God transform you inwardly by a complete change of your mind. Then you will be able to know the will of God — what is good and is pleasing to him and is perfect. Rom. 12:2 GNB

Let your will be liberated from wishes and desires for the things of this world. Immerse your will in the will of God. Every new act of dedication to the will of God effects a change in our nature and thus changes our attitude. In this way alone shall we learn to discern more and more what is good and perfect in the sight of God and pleasing to Him. Then we shall be able to make our decisions according to His will and conduct our lives properly. Therefore, miss no opportunity to surrender yourself to the will of God.

28

Put on the whole armour of God, that you may be able to stand against the wiles of the devil.
Eph. 6:11

You are to put on something — this is a call for action. Claim that which God is offering. He is offering you the victory of Jesus, the redemption He wrought for you. So begin to fight a battle of faith, praising the victorious name of Jesus and

His redeeming blood, and you will be invincible. For he who uses the weapon of faith and prayer will not be overcome by the Enemy.

29

Serve the Lord with gladness!　　　　　Ps. 100:2a

If you find a task or an assignment becoming hard, do it out of love for Jesus. Love will make the most difficult tasks easy for you and at the same time you will be filled with gladness. Work done in love is lovingly accepted by Jesus and it is a joy for Him too.

30

Behold, I stand at the door and knock — so be zealous and repent.　　　　　Rev. 3:20a,19b

Every time others reprove you because of your sins, it is Jesus knocking at the door to your heart and asking you to repent. So humble yourself and turn from your sinful ways. Then you will enter the gate into a new world, where love and zeal will set your heart aflame for Jesus and His kingdom.

31

Seek peace and pursue it.　　　　　1 Pet. 3:11

Are you intent on living in peace with everyone, as far as it lies with you? To pursue peace is to do everything possible to avoid being at odds with anyone. So bring all your obstinacy, pride and bitterness to the cross of Jesus in the firm belief that these sins have been crucified with Him. Then Jesus will pronounce over you the words, 'Blessed are you', for blessed are the peacemakers.

April

Let him who would be loved by God
live in complete obedience
to His commandments.
Then the love of God will be
revealed to him as never before.

1

Let each of us please his neighbour for his good, to edify him.   Rom. 15:2

Your neighbour — at home, at work or in your circle of acquaintances — should be inspired by you, your life and your character to accept Jesus as his Saviour, to love Him and to hate his own sins. He should be inspired to trust God as his Father in all things. The way we live has greater effects than anything else. Practise Christian discipleship in such a way that Jesus can radiate from you; then you will be the best missionary by your example. Take advantage of this opportunity!

2

Don't throw away your trust now — it carries with it a rich reward in the world to come.
                    Heb. 10:35 JBP

In the darkest of nights cling to the assurance that God loves you, that He always has advice for you, a path that you can tread and a solution to your problem — and you will experience what you believe. God never disappoints anyone who places his trust in Him. Indeed, He rewards our trust by giving us His aid here on earth and granting us crowns and thrones in His kingdom above.

APRIL

3

In every thing give thanks.   1 Thess. 5:18 AV

A blessing is contained in *every* thing, for all
things come from the loving hands of God, who
only gives us that which will serve to our good,
even when it is something that is hard for us to
bear. Learn to give thanks for all things, so that
you may receive the blessing that is hidden in
them.

4

*Let us not be desirous of vain glory ... envying
one another.*   Gal. 5:26 AV

By striving for recognition, honours or a leading
position, you stray from Jesus and His path of
lowliness; and spiritual death settles over your
life. Seek to walk in lowliness. For God gives grace
to the humble, and whoever humbles himself will
be lifted up to the heart of God, who will over-
whelm him with His grace and love and let him
partake of divine honours.

5

Be ye not as the horse, or as the mule, which have no understanding: whose mouth must be held in with bit and bridle . . . I will instruct thee and teach thee in the way which thou shalt go: I will guide thee with mine eye. Ps. 32:9,8 AV

Do not insist upon having your own way — it often leads to misery. God must often bridle you with a firm hand to guide you back into His path, His will. Learn to ask first what the will of God is in every situation, in every decision, great or small; for He has the best plan for you in mind. God has promised to reveal His will to you and give you guidance for every decision. Believe in His promise to guide you with His eye. And the more you learn to let Him guide you with His eye as you surrender your will, the more you will experience that His way is always the best.

6

If you cling to your life, you will lose it; but if you give it up for me, you will save it. Matt. 10:39 LB

Have the courage to give up your life and that which makes life worth living to you. Be willing to do so, even when it means making painful breaks and you seem to suffer only loss. If it is truly for Jesus' sake that you suffer loss, then, as surely as God's word is yea and amen, you will experience gain. You will receive the abundant riches of a fulfilled life centred on and stemming from God — and this to such an extent that it will become a visible reality.

7

Do not quench the Spirit. 1 Thess. 5:19

The Spirit of God is a Holy Spirit, who descends from the throne of God and bestows gifts upon the members of the Body of Christ. Take care not to quench the Holy Spirit when He seeks to reveal Himself to you, or through you, or to others, by means of His divine working and bestowal of gifts. If you reject His gifts or speak disparagingly of them when He imparts them to others, you will be guilty of sinning against the Holy Spirit and your fellow Christians. As a result you yourself can forfeit heavenly gifts and blessings, which He could have used to achieve great things in your life.

8

Never pay back . . . an insult with another insult.
1 Pet. 3:9 JBP

When you are reproached, do not react over-sensitively. Do not close your heart to anyone who says unkind things to you; rather, open it wide and seek to open the heart of the other person with humble love. God will then open His heart wide to you and be gracious to you.

9

Let us conduct ourselves becomingly . . . not in quarrelling and jealousy.   Rom. 13:13

Quarrelling and jealousy are enemies of the Kingdom of God. They destroy it and fight against the Lord and King of this kingdom — Jesus, the gentle Prince of Peace. If you want to be God's friend, seek peace even at the expense of your rights and demands. Then your heart and life will be filled with peace, and Jesus will make His dwelling with you.

10

As for those who persist in sin, rebuke them in the presence of all.   1 Tim. 5:20

The Lord, being Light, speaks through His apostle to bid the leaders of the Church to bring sin into the light, without glossing over it. When the offences are exposed by the light before the whole congregation, evil will no longer be able to continue its work in secret. Only he who is prepared to take radical measures in bringing his own sin into the light before all will have the courage to reprove others who sin. In this way the Body of Christ will be cleansed of harmful influences.

11

First take the log out of your own eye, and then you will see clearly to take the speck out of your brother's eye.   Matt. 7:5

How can you be helped — or for that matter your neighbour — when you persist in the most terrible of sins: unwillingness to see that you are in the wrong? Be truthful and admit your guilt. Seek the fault first in your own life. Do so in view of Jesus' words that it is impossible to approach each other in love until, enlightened by the Spirit of God, we have come to see the log in our own eye. Then if your neighbour wrongs you, you will be able, empowered by love and humility, to point out his failings to him in such a way that you do him a real service.

12

Always be thankful.   Col. 3:15b LB

Never forget to give thanks to God — not even on the darkest of days. He is waiting for this. By thanking Him, you will draw His help down and receive new blessings and gifts. The thankful will never lack anything.

13

Whatever gift each of you may have received, use it in service to one another, like good stewards dispensing the grace of God in its varied forms.

1 Pet. 4:10 NEB

Serve with the particular gift that God has graciously bestowed upon you and use it gratefully. Only in this way will God's blessing be upon your ministry. If you perform your ministry in self-will or enviously coveting the gifts of others, it will be fruitless, no matter how successful it may look on the outside.

14

Give glory to the Lord your God before he brings darkness, before your feet stumble. Jer. 13:16

Oppose the advancing powers of darkness and all the Enemy's onslaughts by proclaiming ever anew in prayer and song who God is — the Almighty, the Creator, the God whose name is Yea and Amen and who is omniscient and pure love. Such a testimony glorifies God in these days of ever increasing darkness when He is subjected to more and more disgrace. And you will experience not only that your feet are kept from stumbling, but that light will penetrate the darkness in and about you.

15

Practise hospitality.   Rom. 12:13b

Hospitality often requires sacrifice, but whenever sacrifices are made wholeheartedly, blessings flow — frequently through those to whom you open your home. Above all, however, you will be blessed by Jesus Himself, who comes to you in every guest and who will thank you if you lovingly receive Him in the person of your guest.

16

In the same way urge the young men to be self-controlled.   Titus 2:6 GNB

In all matters great things can be accomplished only if there is self-control. Self-control means curbing one's desires, practising self-denial. In this way we shall become strong. So master your desires in the power of Jesus and His blood, which has been shed for you. Yes, claim the power of His blood. Then you will be able to overcome and you will achieve great things for the Kingdom of God.

17

O fear the Lord, you His saints — revere and worship Him! For there is no want to those who truly revere and worship Him with godly fear.

Ps. 34:9 AB

With each act of dedication to the will of God, by which we reverently and humbly submit to His leadings and actions, we shall become more closely knit to God and our love for Him and the peace in our hearts will grow. Therefore, surrender yourself and your will to God in a spirit of childlike reverence and you will partake of His wealth. Indeed, in His love He will grant you ever anew all that you need.

18

You shall not make wrong use of the name of the Lord your God; the Lord will not leave unpunished the man who misuses his name.   Exod. 20:7 NEB

God's name is holy, because God is holy. But that which is holy can only be mentioned with reverence. If you call upon the name of God in faith, love and reverence, He will incline Himself to you with His grace and aid. But if you misuse the name of God, using it irreverently or lightly, you will just as surely experience that He will withdraw from you and even punish you.

19

Contribute to the needs of the saints.   Rom. 12:13

Regard as holy the saints of God, His own, who testify to Him with their words and lives. Inquire about their needs. Concern is an attribute of the love that God seeks in His children. And we shall one day be judged before the divine seat of judgment as to whether we have practised this love.

APRIL

Take care that love for God's own and concern for their needs are not missing in your life.

20

Cleanse out the old leaven that you may be fresh dough.   1 Cor. 5:7

There is more to cleaning our heart than just being aware of our sins and weaknesses. When we start to clean something, it is a sign that we can no longer stand the filth. So from now on, do not tolerate any of the 'old leaven', the filth of sin, in your heart. It will contaminate your life and bring you under the dominion of Satan. Make a break with sin, so that the life of Christ may gain room in you.

21

See that none of you repays evil for evil, but always seek to do good to one another and to all.   1 Thess. 5:15

To do good to others — whoever they may be and whatever they may have done to you — is your calling as a disciple of Jesus. For Jesus did good to all, including His enemies. To repay evil with evil is the way of the children of this world, which is ruled by Satan. Rather, do good to those who hurt and wrong you. Then you will be pleasing to God and He will show you immeasurable goodness. How many people have you shown goodness to when they hurt you?

22

Therefore I command you, You shall open wide your hand to your brother, to the needy and to the poor, in the land. Deut. 15:11

Do not pass by when you see someone suffering in body or soul. Show concern for him. Open your heart and stretch out your hand to help him. That which you have done to him you have done to Jesus. And one day Jesus will richly reward you and take you into His kingdom.

23

Hope in the Lord! For with the Lord there is steadfast love, and with him is plenteous redemption. Ps. 130:7

On the cross of Calvary you have been set free from your sinful bonds and fetters and the torment they bring. Proclaim the victory of Jesus and His act of redemption ever anew in your prayers, even when you can see no change. Wait steadfastly for the hour when His redemption will also be manifested in you. That hour will come, for Jesus is always greater than all the ensnaring powers of darkness — in your life too.

24

Follow me.   Luke 9:59

With these words Jesus bids you, 'Practise walking in My footsteps, which were marked by humility, disgrace, lowliness, obedience, forgiveness and love. Follow My will and instructions in every situation day by day and not your own will or that of others when it is not in accordance with Mine. Follow My example in the way you live, speak and act.'

Whoever follows Jesus, His wishes and commandments, here on earth, will one day walk at His side in heaven.

25

You must be made new in mind and spirit.
Eph. 4:23 NEB

For every believer it is important that he be constantly renewed by a cleansing process, for the 'soot' of sin settles upon him ever anew. Remove it and take it to the cross of Jesus. The sinner who lies at the foot of the cross filled with contrition will be made new by the blood of the Lamb and receive new blessings from the Spirit of God.

26

*The Lord has told us what is good. What he re-
quires of us is this: to do what is just, to show
constant love, and to live in humble fellowship
with our God.* Mic. 6:8 GNB

God in His goodness has shown us what is good
in His eyes and good for us. Believe Him and trust
that by following His commandment to practise
love and justice, you will have a happy and
meaningful life overflowing with blessings. Therefore, let this commandment be binding for you in
every situation and relationship. As you seek to
live in love, humility and the fear of God by
waging a daily battle of faith and praising the
victory of Jesus, God will embrace you with His
love and bless your path.

27

Rejoice in so far as you share Christ's sufferings.
1 Pet. 4:13

If you want to share in Jesus' glory and kingdom,
commit yourself to sharing His suffering, especially the disgrace, humiliation, scorn, slander
and rejection He still endures. For Jesus they
were the hidden source of His power and glory
— and they will be the same for you. So rejoice
when you are counted worthy to share Jesus'
sufferings. It will bring you the deepest communion with Jesus and inconceivable glory for
eternity.

28

*Work for the Lord with untiring effort and with
great earnestness of spirit.* Rom. 12:11 JB

Open your eyes wide — God may be showing you
an opportunity to serve in His kingdom. He has
a place for everyone, each according to his
strength and abilities. It is not the magnitude of
our task or our gifts, but the zeal, love and devotion with which we do our work that counts.
Those who serve Him with wholehearted dedication will be highly honoured by Him, for tremendous fruit will be reaped one day above by
those who have performed their tasks in loving
dedication to Him.

29

Support the weak. 1 Thess. 5:14 AV

When we support someone else, we are required
to give of our strength. Exert yourself on behalf
of others in love, patience and faith, and you will
be fulfilling God's commandment. Like Christ you
will be laying down your life for the sake of your
brother even if your sacrifice consists of nothing
other than committing yourself in many small
ways to bearing your brother in patience. For
such acts of love and dedication you will be
blessed and repaid a hundredfold.

30

If you are offering your gift at the altar, and there remember that your brother has something against you, leave your gift there before the altar and go; first be reconciled to your brother.

Matt. 5:23f.

If you long to show God your love and worship Him, all your acts of devotion will be of no avail if you are living in irreconciliation. Therefore, go to him against whom you have something or he against you. Do not wait for him to take the first step. Take it yourself and be reconciled with him. Then your prayers will pierce the clouds and have power.

May

Ways of obedience end in joy
and victory, for they are God's ways.
They always lead to Him
and hence to glory.

1

It is hard to stop a quarrel once it starts, so don't let it begin.   Prov. 17:14 LB

If you are involved in a conversation that is not being carried on in a spirit of love, heed the admonition of the Holy Spirit and discontinue it before more unkind words are exchanged and a quarrel starts. Let your main concern be not to transgress against love, even if it means sacrificing your rights and your esteem in the sight of others.

2

Cast all your anxieties on him, for he cares about you.   1 Pet. 5:7

Keep no anxious thought or worry to yourself. Worrying is a pagan attitude. Whoever dwells upon his worries shuts God out of the picture. He lives, plans and reckons without God and His power, love and aid. But God wants to be a Father to you and is waiting for you to bring Him everything that you cannot cope with. Then behold, He will weigh your troubles in His almighty hand and take them into His loving, caring heart. He is always able to help and will do so as surely as He is your Father, who loves you.

3

If any man minister, let him do it as of the ability which God giveth: that God in all things may be glorified through Jesus Christ. 1 Pet. 4:11 AV

Perform your service for the Kingdom of God above all by prayer. The power and authority in your ministry will correspond to your dedication to this hidden ministry of prayer. The more you practise genuine prayer, the more fruit you will bear and the more Jesus Christ will be glorified.

4

Let no one seek his own good, but the good of his neighbour. 1 Cor. 10:24

Do not be preoccupied with yourself, your troubles, cares and wishes. The more you are absorbed by them, the more they will tyrannise you and make you unhappy. Concern yourself with the troubles of your fellow men, and your own troubles will grow small to you. Indeed, you will experience God's help, which He grants to those who help others.

5

Fathers, do not provoke your children to anger, but bring them up in the discipline and instruction of the Lord. Masters . . . forbear threatening.
Eph. 6:4,9

If others are resentful towards you, ask yourself if you are at fault. God stands against you if you have embittered those whom you are supposed to lead and bring up. Ask yourself whether you raise those charged to your care in a spirit of humility, selfless love and meekness — or whether you prefer to domineer and are only seeking your own advantage. Heed the word of the Lord and have done with all threats and anger, so that God will not be angry with you.

6

Let us do good to all men, and especially to those who are of the household of faith.   Gal. 6:10

Whoever does not care for the members of his own household is worse than a pagan. So care for those nearest to you, your brothers and sisters in Jesus Christ; show kindness first of all to them, and be not like a pagan. Also try to help those who are already suffering persecution and martyrdom today because of the Christian faith. Let no opportunity slip by to do good to them and everyone you meet. This will bring you close to Jesus, who shows goodness to all, especially to

His own. So begin to do the same today and your life will become rich and happy.

7

Do not be conformed to this world.   Rom. 12:2

The ways of this world are not the ways of God, but of Satan, the ruler of this world. Therefore, take care that you by no means conform to the trends of the times. Although they are said to be compatible with the present age, they are not compatible with the standards of God. Let your sole guiding principle be the will of God as made known in His commandments, which are not restricted by time, but are valid and binding for all times, since they come from the eternal God Himself. Otherwise, you will not escape the snares set by the ruler of this world.

8

Therefore, my beloved brethren, be steadfast, immovable.   1 Cor. 15:58

You will be immovable if you persevere in faith. Faith is the most powerful weapon in your hand, for your faith is grounded in Him who has defeated death and hell and who is stronger than all things. In the measure that you believe in Jesus' victory, you will experience victory over Satan and all the powers of temptation that seek to make you stray from the one true path that leads to the goal of heavenly glory. So keep faith!

9

Strive for . . . the holiness without which no one will see the Lord. Heb. 12:14

One thing is vital in your brief life on earth and that is whether you are sanctified and transfigured into the image of Jesus. Only then will you be able to behold His countenance in eternity. So strive for holiness, that is, lay aside and hate all that hinders you from attaining this goal. And choose all that will help you to reach this goal, even if it be painful paths of chastening. For such a goal it is worth it.

10

Declare his glory among the nations, his marvellous works among all the peoples! Ps. 96:3

Stop reckoning with normal, human resources! Rather reckon with the almighty hand of God, which performs miracles. Even before your difficulties have been solved, begin to praise His marvellous works in faith. Then you will experience them and be able to witness about them to many.

MAY

11

Live in peace.   2 Cor. 13:11

If you want the peace of God to fill your heart,
then be at peace with your neighbour. In causing
friction, you erect a barrier against the other
person and thus against God. Therefore, offer the
hand of reconciliation to your neighbour ever
anew, and God will offer you His hand, and His
peace will flood your heart.

12

*Like living stones be yourselves built into a spirit-
ual house, to be a holy priesthood, to offer spiritual sacrifices acceptable to God through Jesus
Christ.*   1 Pet. 2:5

God is waiting for sacrifices, which the Holy Spirit
constrains us to make. He is waiting for sacrifices
of body, soul and spirit, since they are an expression of our love and dedication to God and
man. Sacrifice contains life-giving power. When
the flames of sacrifice are blazing, the light of
Jesus is shed abroad, drawing people to Him. Pray
today for the ardour of the Spirit, which will
kindle your love to sacrifice, for only when such
loving sacrifices are made and the grain of wheat
dies, can fruit grow.

96

13

I am the Lord your God . . . You shall have no other gods besides me. Exod. 20:2f. (note)

Because God is Love and because He loves you so much, He makes an absolute demand upon your life. He is your God — your salvation, your deliverance, your protection, your refuge, your Father and your Redeemer. He is to be everything to you. He has an exclusive right to you and can expect you to give your love to nothing and no one' but Him, that is, to have no other gods besides Him. Indeed, He can expect you to love Him above all else. This entails giving Him all your love and wholly surrendering your will to Him, ready to serve Him with your life, your gifts and your abilities. Have you given Him the exclusive right to rule your life? Only then can you be His possession, His child. Remember, your life depends upon this.

14

Do not fear those who kill the body but cannot kill the soul; rather fear him who can destroy both soul and body in hell. Matt. 10:28

Fear God and His verdict over you at the end of your life. It is especially those who call themselves believers that Jesus warns time and again, saying that if they are self-righteous, proud and irreconciled, they could inherit hell and all its horrors for eternity. Let your only fear be that God may

MAY

one day destroy your body and soul in hell, even though you call yourself a believing Christian. Then your worries about suffering in this life, yes, even martyrdom, will grow insignificant to you.

15

We must obey God rather than men.   Acts 5:29

Steps taken in obedience to the Word of God are incontestable. They are always good, for God has taken over the responsibility to bless everyone who acts in obedience to His comandments, as well as all who are affected by such a decision. In every situation, in every decision you have to make, listen to the voice of God and not the voice of your sinful heart nor the voice of men when it contradicts the will of God. Act upon His Word and command. Then a rich blessing will perceptibly rest upon your life.

16

To God be the glory!   Eph. 3:21 GNB

Jesus glorified the Father by trusting Him in the darkest hour and uttering the words, 'Yes, Father.' God is waiting for people who will honour Him not only with their lips, but with the unconditional surrender of their will, as Jesus did. To glorify God in this way honours Him greatly. So give God glory by saying to Him in the darkest hour,

'My Father, I do not understand You, but I trust You.'

17

Let every man be quick to hear, slow to speak, slow to anger.   Jas. 1:19

Remember that our words and anger can have terrible effects upon the hearts of others. Be wary of sinning with quick and heated words. Let Jesus help you, for He alone can deliver you from your bondage to sin. He says, 'I am meek,' and His heart is open to give you that which is His. Come to Him ever anew in contrition and beseech Him to help you, and He will set you free from your vehement and angry disposition, as surely as His name is Redeemer.

18

Let your light so shine before men, that they may see your good works and give glory to your Father who is in heaven.   Matt. 5:16

The glorious light of God, which shines forth radiantly, is His love. So let all your deeds and your very nature be adorned with love, which bears the radiance of heaven. This cannot remain hidden, but will be made manifest and shed abroad. Then others will see the love of God in your deeds and you will receive the most wonderful reward of all: people will give praise and glory to God the Father for your good works and believe in His love.

19

Repent, and believe in the gospel.   Mark 1:15

God is calling you to repentance, for in His love He wants to make you happy. He knows that this can occur only when you repent and turn from your old sinful way of life, which had always caused you heartache, and make a fresh start, following Jesus Christ, who will make your life rich in blessing and fruit. Therefore, turn from your old ways ever anew in the practical matters of everyday life in the power of Jesus' redemption. (See also *Repentance — The Joy-filled Life*)

20

For you have need of endurance, so that you may do the will of God and receive what is promised.
                                        Heb. 10:36

First and foremost seek to do the will of God, no matter how hard and incomprehensible it may seem to you. If, with steadfast patience and endurance, we follow paths in obedience to the will of God, they will end in joy and glory. They will bring us the fulfilment of the tremendous promise: to have close communion with God one day above at His throne.

21

Walk by the Spirit, and do not gratify the desires of the flesh. Gal. 5:16

The gratification of sinful desires destroys one's personality and ruins one's life. Its effects last for the whole span of eternity. God created man in His image and loves each single person, and He does not want us to destroy and defile ourselves. God has our happiness in mind. This is why He bids us, 'Walk by the Spirit. Let your life be ruled by Him. Pray for His guidance. Pray that He will gain dominion in your life.' Then the Holy Spirit will descend and you will experience that He who comes from the throne of God is stronger than your flesh and blood and will grant you victory in your battle against sinful desires.

22

Having purified your souls by your obedience to the truth for a sincere love of the brethren, love one another earnestly from the heart. 1 Pet. 1:22

Let no day go by without sowing love wherever you can — sincere love, which contains no grain of self-interest, earnest love from the heart, which survives when it is put to the test. If you purify your heart and in obedience endeavour to practise this love, God will pour His love upon you now and for all eternity.

MAY

23

Flee from idolatry. 1 Cor. 10:14 AV

Do you have an idol? Do you have a favourite wish or a pet idea that preoccupies your thoughts? Do you have a false attachment to certain possessions or people? Or is your prestige your idol? Then remember that God does not share His love with a person, thing or concept. He will withdraw from you. If you seek the nearness of God, flee from your idols — and God will give Himself and His love to you wholly.

24

Be patient toward all men. 1 Thess. 5:14 AV

Being patient means committing yourself ever anew to bearing that which is hard for you to bear, such as certain ways or mannerisms of your neighbour. Commit yourself to such slight suffering for the sake of the other person. He is worth it, for Jesus suffered death on his behalf. By your patience, you will reflect something of Jesus' nature and you will be able to help your neighbour to find his Lord and to love Him. What a joy that will be to Jesus!

25

*Commit your way to the Lord; trust in him, and
he will act.* Ps. 37:5

Trust God; believe that He is truly almighty, that
He is your loving Father, ever ready to help you.
Trust — and you will have taken the first step
towards the solution of your problems. The second
step will follow. When His time comes, you will
see how He helped you, how He worked everything out and how He turned your sorrow into
joy.

26

*Work hard and willingly, but do it for the sake
of the Lord and not for the sake of men.*
Eph. 6:7 JB

What is the ultimate motivation behind our work,
our ministry? Do we seek to please God and bring
Him joy with our service? We always have the
possibility to do this, for if a task is hard for us
to perform, the love and effort we put into it will
be worth all the more. The harder the task, the
greater God's pleasure will be if we do it willingly
for His sake.

27

Be forbearing with one another, and forgiving, where any of you has cause for complaint: you must forgive as the Lord forgave you. Col. 3:13 NEB

A sign that you have truly forgiven your neighbour is that you have so forgotten what he has done to you that you do not complain about him to others, but speak well of him. Then one day when the Accuser makes accusations against you, God will also speak well of you.

28

Let everyone give as his heart tells him, neither grudgingly nor under compulsion, for God loves the man who gives cheerfully.   2 Cor. 9:7 JBP

If God asks something of you, give it to Him — even if it means making a sacrifice. Sacrifice with a cheerful heart and remember that it is a privilege to be able to fulfil a request for Him who is your heavenly Father, the almighty Creator of heaven and earth. He will thank you for your small sacrifice with His great love and grant you a rich blessing.

29

Let us never tire of doing good.   Gal. 6:9 NEB

Doing good is something we can never overdo, for love is continually constrained to give and do good without ceasing. Nor does love grow weary and give up when hindrances and difficulties arise. You too will learn to love and do good without ceasing if the love of Jesus is really in your heart and shines forth from you.

30

Reprimand the unruly. 1 Thess. 5:14 JBP

An indifferent person can stand by and watch spiritual unruliness destroy the Church of God. But if you consider yourself a member of the Body of Christ, you cannot be indifferent about the 'disease' of another member, which is threatening to destroy his life and infecting the entire Body. So take the ministry of reprimanding seriously. Do not seek the approval of men, but obey the Word of God.

31

Let no one boast of men. 1 Cor. 3:21

When you honour men unduly, showing them excessive love and admiration, because you are falsely attached to them, remember that in doing so you are stealing from Jesus the love and honour that are His due. As a result you will lose His love. For He says, 'I love those who love me.'

June

Since the commandments of God
are born of Him who is Life itself,
they have life-giving power
and impart divine life
to those who obey them.

1

Be filled with the Spirit. Eph. 5:18

It is not sufficient to be born again of the Holy Spirit, to be admonished, guided and comforted by Him. We should be completely filled with Him. Therefore, do not fail to pray the important prayer, 'Fill me with the Spirit.' Whether the Holy Spirit can flow into you in His fullness is of utmost importance for your life and service. Christians empowered by the Spirit are needed in the Kingdom of God — in every fellowship and every family. Therefore, pray for the Holy Spirit to come and you will be filled with Him according to Jesus' promise, 'How much more will the heavenly Father give the Holy Spirit to those who ask him?' (Luke 11:13). (See also *Ruled by the Spirit*)

2

Whoever of you does not renounce all that he has cannot be my disciple. Luke 14:33

Forsake in spirit ever anew that which your heart is attached to on this earth — whether it be people, your job, possessions or other things. Then Jesus, your Lord and Bridegroom, will recognise you as His disciple and take delight in you.

JUNE

3

Drive out the wicked person from among you.

1 Cor. 5:13

Whoever loves Jesus, who died because of our sins, cannot bear evil in his own life, for it still causes Jesus the greatest anguish today. And whoever combats his sins for this reason will take the same approach towards the sins of others. He will not tolerate evil in the Body of Christ and will proceed against those involved — in the spirit of love for Jesus.

4

Be sure of this, that no immoral or impure man, or one who is covetous (that is, an idolator), has any inheritance in the kingdom of Christ and of God.

Eph. 5:5

One question alone is important. 'Where shall I spend eternity?' In the kingdom of death and horror or in the kingdom of light, joy, love, peace and supreme happiness? During your life here on earth you build your dwelling in the next world. Immorality and covetousness are building stones for the kingdom of darkness. Bear this in mind, even if you call yourself a committed Christian. So gather building stones for the Kingdom of God by leading a life of purity, truthfulness, love and goodness. What you sow here on earth you will reap in the next world. (See also *What Comes after Death? — The Reality of Heaven and Hell*)

5

Let us keep awake, with our wits about us.

1 Thess. 5:6 JBP

Do not forget that you are continually in danger of being attacked by the Enemy. He is constantly hovering about your soul, hoping to find a weak spot where he can attack. Therefore, keep awake and equip yourself by frequently calling upon the name of Jesus. In the name of Jesus lies victory and great power. His name carries weight in heaven and hell. Therefore, oppose the Enemy ever anew with this name and you will be victorious.

6

Trust in the Lord with all your heart, and do not rely on your own insight. Prov. 3:5

Childlike trust contains great might. It overpowers the heart of the Father. God the Father cannot disappoint childlike trust. Abandon your 'grown-up' thoughts, plans and worries. Come like a child in full confidence to the Father with all the unsolved problems in your life, and you will experience His aid.

JUNE

7

Show respect for everyone. 1 Pet. 2:17 LB

Despise no man, so that God will not despise you.
Respect everyone as a creation of God bearing
His image, so that God will also respect you.

8

*A hot-tempered man stirs up strife, but he who
is slow to anger quiets contention.* Prov. 15:18

Do not be vehement, hot-tempered or angry, for
your Lord and Saviour is Jesus, the Lamb. Be
gentle, and in your meekness you will have
authority to rule others in the spirit of the Lamb.

9

Test everything; hold fast what is good.
1 Thess. 5:21

You are permitted, indeed, you are expected to
test everything that others say — according to the
words of Holy Scripture, 'You will know them by
their fruits.' However, do not test the words of
others with a prejudiced, critical heart, but with
a humble, loving heart that is receptive for every
blessing that can come to you through others.
And if you do find something amiss, do not reject
everything else as well. Apart from the negative
factors there could be good ones that would be

112

a blessing for you. Don't let such a blessing pass by.

10

Do not continue to live like the heathen, whose thoughts are worthless.   Eph. 4:17 GNB

Ask yourself what fills your thoughts during your work and your spare time and whether your life and thoughts circle round worthless, transient things. Remember how short our time on earth is. Make the most of every day and hour by sowing imperishable seeds of eternal value — for eternity is long and only imperishable seed will yield imperishable fruit.

11

Every athlete exercises self-control in all things.   1 Cor. 9:25

Consider whether you have exercised self-control and denied yourself something to make time for wrestling in prayer and to give your prayers greater emphasis. Consider whether you have let go of people or things in order to give yourself more fully to Jesus, your Lord. And remember that only if you give your full effort, will you attain the goal of glory. What has been your effort so far? Eternity is at stake!

JUNE

12

Therefore comfort one another.   1 Thess. 4:18

Don't pass by someone in need of comfort. Just as you have experienced the comfort of Jesus, God has appointed you to be a comforter for others. Indeed, this is your privilege, for comforting is a heavenly activity. The Holy Spirit is called the Comforter, and God says, 'I am he that comforts you,' because He is Love. To the extent that you truly love your neighbour, you will be able to comfort him in every difficulty and sorrow — especially with words from the Bible, knowing that they have power to speak to a comfortless soul.

13

Avoid every kind of evil.   1 Thess. 5:22 GNB

When you avoid something, you not only sever connections — with a person, for example, or a group of people or a sinful habit — but you flee from it. So flee from every kind of evil. Whoever does not do so has a share in the evil, even if it is only done by others, and will fall under the same judgment. Therefore, avoid evil wherever you may encounter it.

14

Rejoice always.   1 Thess. 5:16

Let us bring joy to Jesus and our fellow men by
showing them a cheerful face. For the Father in
heaven loves to see happy children. So immerse
your face ever anew in the radiance of the love
of Jesus, which emanates from His countenance,
and your face will begin to shine.

15

*Let another man praise thee, and not thine own
mouth; a stranger, and not thine own lips.*
                              Prov. 27:2 AV

When you praise yourself and seek your own
glory, there is no more room left for God to be
praised and glorified. God can only receive praise
and glory from the depths of a humble heart,
empty of its own glory. So make room for God to
be praised by emptying your heart of all self-
praise and self-glorification. Should someone then
find something praiseworthy about you, he will
naturally give glory to the heavenly Father for it.

16

Children, obey your parents in the Lord, for this is right. 'Honour your father and mother' (this is the first commandment with a promise), 'that it may be well with you and that you may live long on the earth.' Eph. 6:1-3

At the judgment seat of Christ the question will be raised, 'How have you treated your parents?' God will ask us whether we have obeyed them and treated them with respect, what kindnesses we have shown them and how we have thanked them. Make use of the time to show your parents goodness as long as you still have them on earth. God promises that He will then bless you and that it will be well with you.

17

Let us therefore cease judging one another.
Rom. 14:13 NEB

Guard yourself against every word of criticism. Such words come from the Accuser in hell and will one day bring us into hell. Judging is like a deadly sword, which we use to strike others down. It is a sin against the sixth Commandment. But love is like the sun, under whose radiance everything begins to blossom. Therefore, look at others with eyes of love and speak with them and about them in the spirit of love.

18

Wait for the Lord, and he will help you. Prov. 20:22

In times of distress, when there seems to be no
way out — whether the struggle be inward or out-
ward — wait expectantly for the hour of help and
deliverance. Blessed are those who wait. Their
waiting will be turned into joy. Those who persevere will experience a blessed fulfilment of their
hopes, both here and in full measure in heaven,
for God will not disappoint our hopes.

19

*Be kind to one another, tenderhearted, forgiving
one another, as God in Christ forgave you.*

Eph. 4:32

Do you wish to abide in the forgiveness of Jesus
Christ? Then never grow weary of showing forgiveness and kindness to your neighbour, even
when you think the limit has been reached. Only
in the measure that you are kind to your neighbour will the kindness of God abide with you and
will you experience His forgiveness ever anew.

20

*First of all, then, I urge that supplications,
prayers, intercessions, and thanksgivings be made
for all men.* 1 Tim. 2:1

On every new day in your life put the most important things first: prayer, thanksgiving and

intercession. Through prayer human hearts will be changed and problems will be solved, which would otherwise have wasted much time. Through prayer strength for body and soul will be given for every task, as well as faith and success. Everything in your life and daily work will become easier; things will fall into place and run more smoothly.

21

Think constantly of those in prison as if you were prisoners at their side. Think too of all who suffer as if you shared their pain. Heb. 13:3 JBP

Do you truly remember them? Today thousands in many countries of the world are being held as prisoners for His name's sake, because they are members of the Body of Christ. We are to remember them as if we and our own family were personally affected. Do you pray and make sacrifices for them? That which you do for one of the least of the brethren you do for Jesus.

22

Do not turn your back on a man who wants to borrow. Matt. 5:42 NEB

Act according to the commandment of love, for love does not turn away from anyone, but always has an open heart for him. When your neighbour requests something from you, encourage him to come to you again the next time he is in need. Let love flow forth from your heart and he will sense that you are open to him and concerned about his requests and needs. For do you not always experience the same with your heavenly Father?

23

But now put them all away: anger, wrath, malice, slander, and foul talk from your mouth.   Col. 3:8

In Jesus Christ you have the opportunity to break with slander, angry remarks, resentful comments and indecent talk. Such manner of speaking brings shame upon Jesus before men. Jesus wants to live in you and gain dominion in you. His redemption is stronger than your old self. Therefore, seize this opportunity by entering a battle of prayer and praising His redemptive blood over your sinful bonds, whatever they may be. Your life should not be a disgrace to you as a Christian nor should it be a disgrace to Jesus; rather it should glorify Him.

24

Let all that you do be done in love.   1 Cor. 16:14

Let your life be 'love in action'. Desire nothing so much as love. It is capable of accomplishing the greatest things on earth for the Kingdom of God and for every human heart. All that you do in love yields fruit and brings peace and a solution to problems. So draw daily from the fount of love, Jesus' heart.

25

Take up the great shield of faith, with which you will be able to quench all the flaming arrows of the evil one.   Eph. 6:16 NEB

When the Enemy attacks you with ever new arrows and you are tempted to capitulate, do not forget to seize the shield of faith, in that you call out the victorious name of Jesus. You will prevail as surely as there is victory in this name, and one day God will crown you as one who returned home from the battle victorious.

26

If any one will not work, let him not eat.
                                                    2 Thess. 3:10

By the sweat of your brow shall you earn your bread, is the command of the Lord. Whoever wishes to eat without having worked is acting against a commandment of God and is, therefore, no longer under His blessing. For idleness breeds iniquity and stands under the judgment of God. Therefore, apply yourself to your work in the name of God with joy and gratitude that you are able and permitted to work. Put all your love and prayers into it. Then your work will emanate the spirit of Jesus and be a blessing for you and others.

27

Be merciful, even as your Father is merciful.

Luke 6:36

Be merciful to your neighbour with his sins and weaknesses. Do not hold them against him. Examine your heart very carefully. Remember that if you are unmerciful, you will forfeit the mercy of God and stand under His judgment rather than His grace. What inconceivable horrors will be our lot if God does not cover us with His mercy!

28

Walk in love, as Christ loved us and gave himself up for us, a fragrant offering and sacrifice to God.

Eph. 5:2

To love is to sacrifice; not just to give up something, but to offer up your self, your life, and whatever makes your life worth living, and to do so out of love as Jesus did. A sign that you truly walk in love is that you are prepared to make sacrifices for your neighbour — sacrifices that cost you something. Do so and God's heart will rejoice that Jesus' sacrifice was not in vain but has won Him disciples.

29

If possible, so far as it lies with you, live at peace with all men.   Rom. 12:18 NEB

Maintain peace with others. Exclude no one from your love. Only when you are at one with all men, as far as it lies with you, will you be taken into the unity of the Holy Trinity as a gift of supreme grace.

30

Pattern your lives after mine ... Our homeland is in heaven.   Phil. 3:17,20 LB

You are called to live with your heart in heaven, in the victory of Jesus Christ and His glory, which He has prepared for you. If you live with this goal ever before you, your present troubles will grow insignificant to you. You will receive the strength to persevere in every hardship and distress, and you will attain the goal of eternal glory at the end of your life like the overcomers who have already completed their course and returned home.

July

By walking in obedience
to the commandments of God,
you cannot go astray, for you
will be held fast and guided
by the very will of God.

1

Let not sin therefore reign in your mortal bodies, to make you obey their passions. Rom. 6:12

Remember that sin lies in wait before the entrance to your heart, continually watching and hoping to find the door slightly open in order to slip in and gain control over your bodily desires. When the door is guarded by prayers and fervent entreaties, by contrition and repentance, sin can find no entrance. So take care that you live a life of daily contrition, repentance and prayer. Then Jesus, and not sin, will reign in you.

2

Give yourselves wholly to prayer and entreaty; pray on every occasion in the power of the Spirit. Eph. 6:18 NEB

A person's body may be covered with sores and ulcers; his ears may hear nothing and his eyes see nothing, and perhaps he can neither sing nor speak with his tongue. And yet if he did nothing else but pray in the power of faith, he would still be able to accomplish the greatest things of all. He could move the arm of God and thus prevail over the whole world and all things. This tremendous opportunity is open to you at every moment, in every situation. Take advantage of it.

3

We know that when he appears we shall be like him, for we shall see him as he is. And every one who thus hopes in him purifies himself as he is pure. 1 John 3:2f.

No one can come before God, the holy Lord, in prayer today without having been cleansed, nor can anyone without cleansing behold His countenance one day in eternity when we shall all be revealed before His holiness. The fire of God's holiness consumes all who are impure. So come to the cross today with all your sins. Cleanse yourself today in the blood of Jesus, the Lamb of God, so that by His redemptive power you will be transformed into His image and prepared for His coming. Take this seriously today, for it could be your last chance. You do not know whether tomorrow will still be yours.

4

Whatever you do, work at it with all your heart, as though you were working for the Lord and not for men. Col. 3:23 GNB

Do not lose yourself in your everyday work and activities. Nor do your work in order to win the approval of others. Rather, lose yourself in God. When you are doing your work, let your innermost heart be centred on Him. Live in His presence, abide in Him, do your work in love for

Him. Then your work will follow you into eternity and you will reap a rich harvest.

5

Count it all joy, my brethren, when you meet various trials. Blessed is the man who endures trial, for when he has stood the test he will receive the crown of life which God has promised to those who love him. Jas. 1:2,12

Make it your aim to serve the Lord with all your heart and be fully at His disposal. But remember, the Enemy will attack and you will be assailed by trials and temptations, because in your service you will snatch away many of his victims. If you endure, calling out the victorious name of Jesus ever anew in the battle of faith, this struggle will earn you the crown of life. So rejoice in trials and temptations.

6

Look at Jesus, whom God sent to be the High Priest of the faith we profess. Heb. 3:1 GNMM

Lift up your eyes to the One who can help you. Help is sure to come. It will come from Him through whom God created heaven and earth and who wrought the act of redemption — Jesus Christ. As the mighty Victor, He has the power to deliver you from all your sins. But there is one

127

thing you must do — look to Him. Then help will come.

7

Have unity of spirit, sympathy, love of the breth-ren, a tender heart and a humble mind. 1 Pet. 3:8

Dismiss the words, 'I don't like him', from your vocabulary and mind, for all people are created in the image of God; they are an offspring of His love, and therefore they are likable and lovable. Pray that God will reveal to you His image in every person, for you are called to help this image come to full development — even in cases where it is no longer visible. God is waiting for your assist-ance in this task.

8

Pray then like this: Our Father who art in heaven.
Matt. 6:9

Are you in great distress? Then say, 'Father, my Father.' Jesus bids you to do so, for as the Son of the Father, He knows what power lies in pro-nouncing and calling upon this name of 'Father'. God will prove Himself to you according to the way you draw near to Him and call upon Him. If you turn to Him as the Father, you will ex-perience that He is a true Father, whose nature it is to care for His child, to embrace him lovingly, smooth the way for him and send him aid. So do as Jesus says and you will taste the Father's love as His child.

9

Use the present opportunity to the full, for these are evil days.   Eph. 5:16 NEB

As the days grow increasingly evil, it is evident that Satan is at work all the more, making the most of time. This calls for a complete dedication on our part to use the time available in our short lives on earth to build up the kingdom of Jesus. What have you given in the way of time, energy and money for the building up of Jesus' kingdom and the saving of souls? What have you done, so that Jesus might receive honour and love? Take advantage of the time and make the most of every opportunity to sow seeds for His kingdom.

10

Love is not selfish.   1 Cor. 13:5 GNB

Deny yourself and say to your ego with all its demands, 'I do not know you, nor do I want to know you.' And God will acknowledge you and concern Himself about you, and so will your fellow men.

JULY

11

Be alert; stand firm in the faith; be valiant and strong. 1 Cor. 16:13 NEB

You can never allow yourself a holiday from the battle of faith, for Satan is fighting without pause to gain your soul. So do not tire of battling. Take up the weapon of the prayer of faith anew. For only he who battles can be a victor and only victors receive the crown.

12

In the day of prosperity be joyful, and in the day of adversity consider; God has made the one as well as the other. Eccles. 7:14

Even on the darkest days God is waiting for you to trust His love, which lies behind everything. At such times the stars of promise like 'I will never fail you nor forsake you' shine the brightest. Gaze at these stars, cling to the promises in faith, and you will emerge from the dark days as victor, having stood the test.

13

Put off your old nature . . . and put on the new nature, created after the likeness of God in true righteousness and holiness. Eph. 4:22,24

You cannot put on new clothes without first removing the old ones. Likewise there is no possibility for Jesus to renew you unless you first bring Him your old nature to be cleansed by the blood of the Lamb, and lay down your old clothes at the feet of those whom you have hurt, by humbling yourself beneath your sins and asking for forgiveness. Then Jesus will clothe you with the new garment of His nature.

14

For the sake of the Lord submit to every human authority. 1 Pet. 2:13 GNB

Though Son of God, Jesus was subject to His parents. If you want to be a disciple of Jesus Christ, submit to those who are placed in authority above you, unless you are required to do something that is against the Word of God. Practise obedience, so that God's promise of grace for those who keep His commandments will also hold true for you.

15

Confess your sins to one another. Jas. 5:16

Confess to God, but also to people, 'Yes, I have sinned against heaven and against this or that particular person.' And you will hear the heavenly Father say, 'Bring him the best robe and a ring for his finger.' He will embrace you and you will receive forgiveness from God and men and go your way rejoicing.

16

Put to death . . . ruthless greed which is nothing less than idolatry.   Col. 3:5 NEB

The desire to have more than that which God had given was the first sin — and it cost mankind paradise. Take care that it does not also cost you paradise. Be content with the necessities of life that you have received from the hands of God. Surrender all your selfish desires to God, so that they might be put to death ever anew on the cross of Jesus. And He will shower you ever anew with His heavenly blessings and gifts, which will make your heart happy and content.

17

Ye that love the Lord, hate evil.   Ps. 97:10 AV

Whoever is a true disciple of Jesus rejoices in all that is pure, good and noble and hates that which Jesus hates — every form of sin, injustice and lawlessness. Instead of just sadly realising the evil in yourself and others, begin to hate it and fight against it. In so doing, you will demonstrate your love to Jesus and bring joy to His heart.

18

Thou shalt not commit adultery.   Exod. 20:14 AV

God has ordained the covenant of marriage as a reflection of the covenant of love that He has made with mankind and that He maintains steadfastly. To break a marriage covenant after having entered it with solemn vows will inevitably have serious consequences. It is a breach of truth, love and faithfulness. One deceives the person with whom one made the covenant and sins against him. Sin, however, cries out to heaven and calls down God's judgment and punishment. Hold sacred the covenant of marriage, so that the wrath of God will not burn against you, but rather His blessing come upon you and your family.

19

Do not become proud, but stand in awe.

Rom. 11:20

Nothing is to be feared more than having God against us. For he whom God opposes seeks in vain for help — he is at the mercy of every hardship and distress. Beware of your pride and arrogance, which make God stand against you. Humble yourself beneath the mighty hand of God when He strikes you — also when He uses others as His instruments — in order to bring you down from your false sense of superiority. Then God will be for you, and your prayer for help will be heard.

20

O give thanks to the Lord, for He is good; for His mercy and loving-kindness endure for ever.

Ps. 106:1 AB

Childlike thanks ties the bond of love between you and God the Father. So give much thanks — indeed, let no day pass by without giving thanks. Then you will become more closely knit to God — your trust in God the Father and your love for Him will grow.

21

Endure what you suffer as being a father's punishment. God does it for our own good, so that we may share his holiness. Heb. 12:7,10 GNB

It is worthwhile enduring in patience, for the gain is very great. You are to share God's holiness, His nature, and this will enable you to behold Him one day. So whenever you have to suffer discipline, fix your eyes firmly on the goal of heavenly glory, for which the chastenings are supposed to prepare and transfigure you. When you consider eternity, your suffering will seem small to you.

22

Enter by the narrow gate. Matt. 7:13

Be willing to follow hard and narrow paths, which do not allow you any freedom to do as you please, nor give you any room to fulfil your desires. And on these narrow paths you will find your heart's deepest desire and fulfilment for your life. For here you will find the One who is abundant Life — Jesus.

23

You must abstain from fornication; each one of you must learn to gain mastery over his body, to hallow and honour it, not giving way to lust . . . because . . . the Lord punishes all such offences.

1 Thess. 4:4,6 NEB

Live and act in the awareness of the presence of God, who is your Judge, for His eyes see you at all times and you cannot hide from His holiness and His judgment, which will descend upon those who live in sexual immorality and yield to lust. Choose the path of purity. Jesus redeemed you on the cross, so that you could walk this path. Follow it, for only then will you become happy.

24

Do not let the sun go down on your anger.

Eph. 4:26

Do everything within your means to settle any discord or hostility between you and another person before the end of the day, even if obstacles seek to frustrate your intention and the Enemy whispers to you, 'It can wait till tomorrow.' Only

135

JULY

he who lives according to this commandment will experience that the sun of mercy will never set upon him, for God is gracious to those who forgive.

25

He who does not take his cross and follow me is not worthy of me. Matt. 10:38

Willingly take up the cross ever anew. It is a sign that you love Jesus when you want to follow the way of the cross with Him. Believe that hidden in the cross is glory, which awaits you one day in eternity. The fruit and harvest you reap will correspond to how much you love your cross and lovingly embrace it. Even here on earth you will taste the love of Jesus in the same measure that you bear your suffering and cross.

26

Yield yourselves to God as men who have been brought from death to life, and your members to God as instruments of righteousness.
Rom. 6:13b

By grace God raised you to divine life, which is love, peace and joy. Live this life and demonstrate it by using your bodily members to the honour of God. In this way you will show your love to Him. If you live in total submission to God's will, to His commandments, you can be a living instru-

136

ment of His righteousness for His service and bear fruit for Him.

27

Do not grumble, brethren, against one another, that you may not be judged; behold, the Judge is standing at the doors. Jas. 5:9

Even grumbling against someone else is a sin and will incur judgment. For at the bottom of grumbling and complaining about others is the spirit of criticism and unlovingness. Do you measure your actions against the standard of God? Instead of criticising your brother, criticise yourself, your impatience, your lack of love and your unwillingness to bear others. And love your brother in such a way that he will return to the right path.

28

Rejoice with those who rejoice. Rom. 12:15

Show a loving concern for your neighbour. Rejoice with him; weep with him. Then God's heart will be opened to you and weep with you when you are in sorrow, and Jesus will share your joy with you and increase it.

29

You should set your hearts on the highest spiritual gifts. 1 Cor. 12:31 JBP

Only he who sets his heart on something will attain it. This also applies to such significant things as the gifts of the Holy Spirit. Heed the challenge of the Word of God. The failure to follow a divine summons will have serious consequences for all eternity. So act upon His word and ask for the gifts of the Spirit. Then you will be enriched, equipped and empowered for your ministry.

30

Since Christ suffered and underwent pain, you must have the same attitude he did; you must be ready to suffer. 1 Pet. 4:1 LB

Don't try to escape suffering; rather give yourself to it, for tears mark the earthly path of God's elect. But blessed are those who weep here, for one day they will laugh and be filled with joy beyond measure.

31

Whatever you do, in word or deed, do everything in the name of the Lord Jesus, giving thanks to God the Father through him. Col. 3:17

Great might lies in the name of Jesus. And whatever is done in His name has power. So call upon the name of Jesus before you begin your work or other activities, and give thanks that you may claim this name. In this name there is aid for every situation, there is deliverance and victory.

August

Love proves its genuineness
by obeying the commandments of
God, for love seeks to do the will
of the one it loves.

1

In humility count others better than yourselves.
Phil. 2:3

Count others in your family, at your job and at your church as better than yourself by approaching them in the awareness that you are not worthy to receive their kindness. Then the Lord will regard your lowliness, and your fellow men, too, will be kind to you.

2

When you give a dinner or a banquet, do not invite your friends or your brothers or your kinsmen or rich neighbours, lest they also invite you in return, and you be repaid. But when you give a feast, invite the poor, the maimed, the lame, the blind, and you will be blessed, because they cannot repay you. You will be repaid at the resurrection of the just.
Luke 14:12—14

Invite those who cannot repay your kindness — those who are strange or even repulsive to you, because they are unfortunate, ugly or poor. Open wide the door of your heart and the door of your home to them, and God will open wide for you the door to His glory.

143

3

If you would enter life, keep the commandments.
Matt. 19:17

Let us remember that our life — our happiness or unhappiness — depends upon our attitude to the commandments of God. God hates evil, because He is Goodness, because He knows that evil causes us harm and brings about our ruin. His love wants to lead us, by means of His commandments, along the path of happiness. So act according to His commandments in the power of Jesus' redemption and your life will be filled with meaning and joy.

4

Keep your life free from love of money, and be content with what you have. Heb. 13:5

This is a call to be taken seriously. When your needs are adequately supplied, according to your circumstances, be content. This is a commandment of Scripture. So renounce all desire for more. By following His commandments, you will be on the right path. On this path alone will Jesus be with you and be able to fulfil His promises in your life.

5

You shall worship the Lord your God and him only shall you serve. Matt. 4:10

Have no other gods besides God, your Lord, for He is a jealous and holy God, zealous for His own and He hates divided love. Love Him, serve Him exclusively and honour Him. Then He will love you in return as though you were the only person in the world. He will bless you and your work in all eternity.

6

Let a man examine himself. 1 Cor. 11:28

Before you examine and judge others, first examine your own words, actions and attitude. Only when you have received light about yourself and your own weaknesses, can you examine and form a proper opinion about others. Judge yourself and then you will see others in the light of God's merciful love, in which you yourself find mercy.

7

Do not be deceived: 'Bad company ruins good morals.' 1 Cor. 15:33

Beware! Satan, the Tempter, uses people as his instruments. Naivety is dangerous when someone is lying in wait to trap us, having the perdition of our soul in mind. Search your heart and ask yourself if there is anyone you associate with who could be an instrument of the Enemy, seeking to lead you astray. Ask yourself whether your conversations — and those you listen to — are right in the sight of God. Then act and make a break with everyone who could harm your soul.

8

Kill everything in you that belongs only to earthly life: fornication, impurity, guilty passion, evil desires. Col. 3:5 JB

Killing is the most ruthless procedure there is. This means being hard on yourself with regard to every evil desire in your flesh. Take measures against them. Don't give them the smallest breathing space. For the judgment of divine wrath will descend upon those who serve sin in their bodies.

9

Do good to those who hate you. Luke 6:27

God will ask you one day, 'Have you done good to those who hated you and made life hard for you?' Such acts of kindness are a sign that you are able to love. If they are missing in your life, you are a mere 'nothing' according to 1 Corinthians 13. But if you show love to those who make life difficult for you, God will pour out His love upon you. He will treat you kindly as a child who bears his Father's traits and acts in His spirit.

10

Take your share of suffering as a good soldier of Christ Jesus. 2 Tim. 2:3

Jesus seeks people who are willing to take their share of suffering. They are the best soldiers for His kingdom. It was by suffering, not by working, that Jesus victoriously wrought our redemption. Suffering accomplishes far more than all our activities, which may even give us much satisfaction. So say Yes to the suffering in your life. Then you will accomplish great things and reap a rich harvest in eternity.

11

Seek the Lord, all you humble of the land, who do his commands; seek righteousness, seek humility; perhaps you may be hidden on the day of the wrath of the Lord. Zeph. 2:3

God's judgment of wrath will soon erupt over mankind, because man's sins are crying out to heaven. But the force with which the judgment will descend upon a country depends on whether God can still find Christians who walk in humility and live according to His commandments. What a great responsibility is, therefore, placed in your hands if you consider yourself to be a child of God! Be mindful of this responsibility. Be humble towards all in everyday life and live according to Jesus' commandment to love and bear your

147

neighbour in the same way that Jesus loves and bears you.

12

Judge not, and you will not be judged.   Luke 6:37

Unless your duty requires it, do not utter a word of criticism or disapproval about anyone. It could bring you under the condemnation of God. Instead, judge yourself — and one day you will go free at the judgment.

13

No man must overreach his brother in business (or in lawsuits) or invade his rights, because, as we told you before with all emphasis, the Lord punishes all such offences.   1 Thess. 4:6 NEB (note)

Have you gone along with the 'customary' practices of modern-day business life and competition? All such offences are noted by God and registered for the day of His righteous judgment. It will be a terrible thing to fall into the hands of the living God when He reveals Himself to you as the God of wrath and vengeance because of your unforgiven offences. So remove from your life today all that provokes the wrath of God.

14

Repent therefore, and turn again, that your sins may be blotted out, that times of refreshing may come from the presence of the Lord.   Acts 3:19

Remember, God gives sinners an opportunity to repent. So you are not lost in your sins and a burden to God and man. You can be a bringer of joy if you turn from your old ways in contrition and receive the forgiveness of Jesus. For there is joy in heaven over every sinner who repents.

15

Do not become slaves of men.   1 Cor. 7:23

Do not live, speak or act to please people, for then you deprive your life of its power. Be royally independent of their praise and criticism. Be Christ's servant and take care that you have God's approval. Then you can bless many and, having been His servant, you will one day stand at His side above.

16

I give you a new commandment: love one another; as I have loved you, so you are to love one another.   John 13:34 NEB

Begin to love this commandment as the most precious legacy of Jesus and His request to you. Then it will be easy for you to follow it, for love makes even the hardest things easy and sweetens everything.

17

Never act from motives of rivalry or personal vanity.   Phil. 2:3 JBP

God is asking you what the real motives are behind your work and your service for the Kingdom of God. Let all your activities — including your religious activities for the Kingdom of God — come under the all-revealing light of the Holy Spirit ever anew, so that all self-centredness and desire for recognition will be laid bare. Claim the redemptive power of the blood of Jesus, so that all that you do may be done purely out of love for Jesus and may stand before God one day, since it was performed with the pure motive of glorifying Him.

18

Thou shalt not kill.   Exod. 20:13 AV

God created man in His own image and breathed into him the breath of life. To take a person's life, and this includes unborn life, is to encroach upon God's rights. If we do so, we provoke His greatest wrath and bring down His judgment upon us. And if you think that there is no danger of your committing such a crime, be wary of 'words that can kill' and tremble before God in holy fear. If you utter such words against your brother, it can cost you your life, that is, eternal life, as Jesus says in the Sermon on the Mount.

19

Bring the full tithes into the storehouse, that there may be food in my house; and thereby put me to the test, says the Lord of hosts, if I will not open the windows of heaven for you and pour down for you an overflowing blessing.   Mal. 3:10

Should you not make generous sacrifices to God, who so richly bestows gifts upon you daily? Ask yourself whether it is your meagre sacrifices that are causing God to withhold His gifts. God acts exactly according to His word and He will open the windows of heaven over you when you give Him the full tithe of your income for the needs of His kingdom.

20

Love is not resentful.   1 Cor. 13:5

In spirit give the kiss of love ever anew to those whose personality and ways are hard for you to bear, and your resentment will disappear. Indeed, you will experience that God will give you the kiss of love ever anew.

151

AUGUST

21

Lead a life worthy of the Lord, fully pleasing to him.   Col. 1:10

Live with the one aim: that your life may be pleasing to God. Follow in Jesus' footsteps along the path of humility and obedience; moreover, humble yourself ever anew beneath your failings and sins. In doing so, you will have God's approval and when you have this, you have everything you need. Then you can be sure of His love and care for you and know that your prayers will be answered, just as God has promised to those who 'keep his commandments and do what pleases him' (1 John 3:22b).

22

Let each of you look not only to his own interests, but also to the interests of others.   Phil. 2:4

God has given you a wonderful commission — a commission of love: to look to the interests of your neighbour and to help him attain that which could be beneficial to him. If you love and care for your neighbour in this way, even at the expense of your own interests, you will fulfil Jesus' commandment of love, which contains the greatest promises for your life in time and eternity.

23

Don't criticize and speak evil about each other, dear brothers. If you do, you will be fighting against God's law of loving one another, declaring it is wrong . . . What right do you have to judge or criticize others? Jas. 4:11f. LB

If you speak evil of a brother, you treat him like an enemy. What judgment then will Jesus, who commands us to love our enemies, pronounce upon us if we do not even love our brother, but presume to criticise him with our words and treat him like our enemy! An unmerciful judgment will be pronounced over us on the day of judgment.

24

Whatever you do, do all to the glory of God.
1 Cor. 10:31

Only a life that is motivated by the one desire, 'God must be glorified in all that I do,' is worth living. So perform even the smallest and most insignificant tasks with this loving intention. And there will be no end to the fruit awaiting you in eternity.

25

Husbands, love your wives, as Christ loved the church and gave himself up for her. Wives, be subject to your husbands, as to the Lord.

Eph. 5:25,22

The holy calling of marriage is to reflect the relationship between the Church and the Lord Jesus. Let marriage partners, then, love each other with mutual reverence and respect. When you conduct your married life in such a way, you will bring joy to God and a rich blessing to your family. Yes, let it be a visible testimony in this age when God's directives about marriage are so often disregarded.

26

Walk as children of light.   Eph. 5:8

Ask God daily to place the sins you are not aware of in the light of His countenance, so that you might see them. The more you recognise your sin and turn from the darkness as a child of light, the more you will see into the depths of His merciful heart, and you will experience mercy and deliverance.

154

27

You shall remember all the way which the Lord your God has led you. Deut. 8:2

Do not forget to set time aside daily to remember all the good things that God has done for you. Such a time of remembrance will bring you God's blessing and cause your trust in Him to grow strong, so that you will more than overcome in your difficulties and battles.

28

If any of you lacks wisdom, let him ask God who gives to all men generously. Jas. 1:5

The wisdom of this world is deceptive, since it comes from the prince of this world. You are offered divine wisdom, which is granted to the poor and to those who are foolish in the eyes of the world and despised by man, but who expect and seek everything from God the Father — including true wisdom. Today more than ever God wants us to ask for His wisdom, so that His children might resist the powers of deception. Ask, and not only will you receive divine wisdom, but you will also taste heaven.

29

But for your part, stand by the truths you have learned. 2 Tim. 3:14 NEB

With every new trend of the times another item of the heritage of our faith is declared invalid. Remember that Satan, the prince of this age, is behind it. Bit by bit he is undermining the validity of Holy Scripture, including the commandments themselves. But if you lose part of the Word of God, you lose the eternal life it contains.

30

Abhor that which is evil; cleave to that which is good. Rom. 12:9 AV

Do not sympathise with that which is evil in a false sense of brotherly love. Abhor it, just as God hates and punishes sin. Cleave to that which is good, for God is Goodness and all that comes from Him is good. Do you belong to God? If so, you will endeavour to practise whatever is good and hate evil in whatever form it presents itself, abhorring it as something which belongs to hell and Satan and which requires your wholehearted resistance.

31

Let your hearts overflow with thankfulness.

Col. 2:7 NEB

Always express thanks for the smallest services and kindnesses you receive from others — and one day God will thank you for the smallest services and tokens of love that you have given Him.

September

Paths of obedience are worth more
than words of faith,
for obedience is faith in action.

1

Love in all sincerity. Rom. 12:9 NEB

If you don't want to be a pharisee, then ask your-self whenever you read a passage of Holy Scrip-ture or make a statement — especially when it concerns love — whether it has resulted in action in your life. Only love that comes from the heart of God is sincere and unfeigned. So take care that you maintain a living relationship to the heart of God and that your love is sincere. Only then will you belong to the truly loving souls who will one day enter the City of God.

2

Put your trust in the Lord, and offer him pleasing sacrifices. Ps. 4:5 LB

Give yourself and your life wholly and unreserved-ly to God. Only if you lead a life of total dedication and implicit trust, will you experience God's over-flowing love, His aid and His miracles in abun-dance. So sacrifice everything including the things to which you cling. He is waiting for you to do so today.

3

Let marriage be held in honour among all ... for God will judge the immoral and adulterous.

Heb. 13:4

Marriage is sacred to God, and therefore it is to be held sacred. Let everyone who is guilty of the sin of adultery — according to Jesus' standard in the Sermon on the Mount — be willing to undergo judgment in this life, so that he will not be condemned one day in eternity. Let him bring his sins into the light by confessing them to a spiritual counsellor; let him be cleansed of them in the blood of the Lamb and let him turn from his sinful ways. The grace of God still avails when one submits to such judgment today, but it will be terrible to fall into the hands of the living God one day in eternity as an impenitent sinner.

4

Lay up for yourselves treasures in heaven.

Matt. 6:20

Loving your neighbour, denying self, relinquishing earthly goods, following Jesus uncompromisingly, bearing the cross — these are all treasures that have value in heaven. If you lay up such treasures during your short earthly life, you will inherit immeasurable wealth at your homecoming above.

5

Charge them before the Lord to avoid disputing about words, which does no good. 2 Tim. 2:14

Disputes about Scripture are forbidden territory. Do not venture into such territory; you will only be diverted from your goal. It is the Holy Spirit who will help you to understand the mysteries of God in Holy Scripture, and God gives the Holy Spirit to those who love Him. Instead of arguing, learn to love God more, and His Spirit will show you the answer to your questions.

6

Forgive one another, as God has forgiven you through Christ. Eph. 4:32 GNB

Forgive with all your heart those who wrong you, for you yourself have wronged others and must ask forgiveness of God and your fellow men ever anew. Blessed are those who forgive, for they shall be forgiven.

7

Cursed is he who does the work of the Lord with slackness. Jer. 48:10

To be slack in doing your work for God is not merely a flaw in your disposition, but a sin — indeed, a provocation of God, who is a consuming Fire. Jesus said, 'I have come to cast fire upon the earth.' So if you don't want to stand under the curse of God, spend yourself for His kingdom. Heed neither opposition, suffering, humiliation, disgrace nor wounds that you might incur in the process. And in heaven above there will be no end to the fruit that you reap when your works follow you.

8

Submit to God and accept the word that he plants in your hearts, which is able to save you.
Jas. 1:21 GNB

Do not rebel when you are convicted by the Word of God, nor brush it aside. Rather, let your conscience be struck and bear willingly the pain of being judged. Only then will His Word be able to bring forth fruit in your life, and, instead of condemning you in eternity, serve towards the salvation of your soul.

9

Owe no one anything, except to love one another.
Rom. 13:8

Never withhold love from your neighbour. If you withhold this, you withhold everything. If you give him the love you owe him, you give him everything — and God will pour out His love upon you and richly reward you.

10

Thou shalt not covet.   Exod. 20:17 AV

Do not feed evil desires in your heart by toying
with thoughts of possessing that which belongs to
someone else. When the first thought of covetousness passes through your mind, call upon the
victorious name of Jesus, so that the Enemy, who
seeks to make you sin, will be silenced.

11

*Therefore, while the promise of entering his rest
remains, let us fear lest any of you be judged to
have failed to reach it.*   Heb. 4:1

It often happens that when a person stands at the
end of a long line of people, the door closes just
before his turn. Take care that you do not fall to
the end of the line in your spiritual life. Rather be
willing to let it cost you something to reach the
eternal goal. Otherwise, the door to glory may be
closed to you. Only those souls that pursue holiness attain it. So make holiness your aim.

12

*Therefore put away all filthiness and rank growth
of wickedness.*   Jas. 1:21a

Put away, that is, break with filthy thoughts and
have no more to do with them. God can give you
a new mind only when you can no longer bear the

old one in all its impurity. The decision lies in your hands. But woe betide him who, in a filthy state of mind, shamelessly dares to appear before the holy countenance of God!

13

Submit yourselves therefore to God. Resist the devil and he will flee from you. Jas. 4:7

Submit your will to the will of God. Surrender yourself fully to Him and humble yourself beneath His mighty hand. You will then be able to withstand the devil in the best possible way, for he flees when he sees a truly humble soul.

14

Whoever would be great among you must be your servant. Mark 10:43

Be of service to everyone, including the lowly, so that you may be present at Jesus' table one day when He girds Himself and serves those who humbled themselves on earth, but have now been raised up to His throne.

15

Do not refuse a kindness to anyone who begs it, if it is in your power to perform it. Prov. 3:27 JB

Satan is the 'Refuser' and incites us to refuse when a request is made of us, when a sacrifice, a service or some form of assistance is required of us. God, on the contrary, is always willing to help. So entreat Jesus to create in you a willing spirit, so that you no longer refuse to help. Remember, Jesus Himself, in the person of the one in need, is making the request of you. Refuse Him nothing. Otherwise you will deeply regret it.

16

Let the peace of God rule in your hearts.

Col. 3:15 AV

Close your heart when agitation, irritation, anger or indignation try to force their way in and create turmoil. Bar the entrance with the name of Jesus. Say, 'Jesus, You are my Peace.' Say this again and again; then His peace will fill your heart and the turmoil will die down.

17

Watch ... and pray lest the Tempter overpower you.

Mark 14:38 LB

There is no condition more dangerous than that of sleepiness. Only when you are awake, can you wage a battle. So be on the alert and fight, for only when there has been a battle, can your life speak of victory. And the victors, the overcomers, are those who will be shown great honour and glory when they enter heaven.

167

18

Let every one speak the truth with his neighbour.
Eph. 4:25

You belong to Jesus, who is the Truth, only when you speak the truth. Every kind of falsehood, including a 'white lie', separates you from Him and binds you to Satan, who was a liar from the beginning. Therefore, bring even the smallest lie in your life into the light by confessing it before God and man, so that it may be blotted out by the forgiveness of Jesus. Always choose the truth, so that Jesus, the King of truth, may rule in your heart.

19

Have this mind among yourselves, which you have in Christ Jesus, who ... emptied himself.
Phil. 2:5,7

Whoever loves Jesus will want to share His pathway and be poor in possessions, gifts and treasures for body and soul. Therefore, you will love poverty as much as you love Jesus, who lived a life of poverty. Hold sacred the treasure of poverty, for only the poor are richly endowed with God's gifts. To them He grants the treasures of His heavenly kingdom and reveals His heart of love.

20

Keep alert as you pray, giving thanks to God.

Col. 4:2b GNB

Is it a struggle for you to pray? Do your prayers seem lifeless to you? There is a way to revive your prayer life. Begin to give thanks for everything in your life for which you owe God thanks. And if you have any needs that you have asked God to supply, in accordance with His promise, give thanks in advance that He will hear your prayers. Give thanks as if you had already received — in the assurance that His promises are yea and amen and that He will act upon them. Such thanksgiving will cheer your heart, bring new life to your prayers and draw down God's grace upon you.

21

Show a gentle attitude towards everyone.

Phil. 4:5 GNB

Do not be gentle and kind only to those whom you are fond of. This will bring you no reward. Show love and kindness also to those whom you find difficult to get along with. Yes, let everyone, without distinction, sense your gentleness and kindness — and your reward will be great in heaven.

SEPTEMBER

22

Neither should we give way to sexual immorality
as did some of them, for we read that twenty-three
thousand fell in a single day!   1 Cor. 10:8 JBP

Your body is the temple of God. Thus it is not left
to your discretion what you do with it. Sexual
immorality, the Lord says, is a sin that leads to
death if it is not repented of. And He has given
a shattering example in the history of His people.
So make a complete break with such sins.

23

Be not forgetful to entertain strangers: for thereby
some have entertained angels unawares.
                                        Heb. 13:2 AV

Forgetfulness is also a sin. One can simply forget
that one should open his home and offer hospitality to a guest whenever the occasion arises. If we
are so unloving and preoccupied with ourselves,
we may fail to take in angels and thereby forfeit
many blessings. So open your home and pray for
a love that has a perceptive eye and an attentive
ear for the requests of others, and one day God

the Father will open His house and take you home
to Himself.

24

*Ascribe to the Lord the glory of his name; worship
the Lord in holy array.*   Ps. 29:2

Forget yourself, your prestige and your desire to
make a name for yourself. Let your thoughts revolve round the Lord and worship Him for who
He is — the Creator, the Almighty, the Judge of
the whole world, the omniscient Lord, the loving
Father, who cares for us, guides us and raises us
as His children.

Let your thoughts circle round Jesus, the mighty
Redeemer, the triumphant Lamb, the risen Lord
and Prince of Victory, the returning King and
Bridegroom.

Let your thoughts revolve round the Holy Spirit
and worship Him as the Creator Spirit, who gives
new birth to men, the Spirit who teaches us to be
children of the Father, the Spirit of power and
might, the Counsellor and Comforter.

Revolve round God, His glory and His name in
this way. Enter into His presence, arrayed in the
garment of humility. In worshipping and giving
thanks, you will come to know Him better and
partake of the nature of God. And you will be
granted strength and joy in abundance.

25

If your right eye causes you to sin, pluck it out and throw it away. Matt. 5:29

Whenever the leprosy of sin can be found in your nature, take measures and 'pluck out your eye'. For sin spreads like cancer. Whoever does not spare himself in the battle against sin will be spared by God on the day of His judgment.

26

Show mercy and kindness and tender compassion every man to his brother. Zech. 7:9b AB

Let no harsh word proceed from your mouth, for an unmerciful judgment will be passed on the hard-hearted. But blessed are the merciful, for they shall obtain mercy.

27

It is these very things [immorality, impurity and covetousness] which bring down the wrath of God upon the disobedient. Have nothing to do with men like that. Eph. 5:6f. JBP

What kind of company do you keep? Do you associate with people who love God and whose lives bear the traits of Jesus or with those whose lives are marked by immorality, impurity, covetousness or love of money and who stand under the wrath of God? His wrath will also come upon you if you do not part company with them. Therefore, cease to cover up sin, so that you may partake of His grace.

28

Repent, for the kingdom of heaven is at hand.
Matt. 4:17 AV

Repent daily, and you will daily have a foretaste of heaven. Repent abundantly, and you will partake abundantly in the kingdom of heaven.

29

My son, despise not the chastening of the Lord; neither be weary of his correction. Prov. 3:11 AV

Do not be despondent when the way is hard. When God takes pains to chasten and discipline you, it is a sign of how much He loves you and yearns to impart His glory to you. He chastens you in order to transform you into His image. When you have experienced release from the bondage of sin, you will become happy and make others happy in turn and one day attain the goal of glory. So thank the Father for all the trouble He takes with you, and your hard path will become easy for you.

30

Do not be proud, but accept humble duties.

Rom. 12:16 GNB

He who is humbled here before God and man will one day wear a crown. So do not strive for superiority, recognition and distinction, for important positions and commissions. Bring this yearning, which springs from self-love, ever anew to the cross, for it must die — no matter how painful it is — if you are to reflect Jesus, who was a servant of all.

October

The commandments of God are not
to be fathomed by the human mind.
Rather, they are to be accepted
and carried out by the will.
Often it is not until afterwards
that we see how wise they were.

1

Let your manner of life be worthy of the gospel of Christ. Phil. 1:27

What do our lives and actions speak of? If they speak of joy, love and peace, then the Gospel, the Good News, shines forth. Jesus, who has given you full salvation, expects this from your manner of life, so that you can testify to the world of your Lord and His message. By the testimony of your life others are to come to believe in Him.

2

So you also must consider yourselves dead to sin and alive to God in Christ Jesus. Rom. 6:11

A sign that you truly died with Christ to sin when you gave your life to Him is that you do not readily give sin a new right to live. Each time sin takes you unawares, bring it into the light immediately and thus to the cross where your old man is given up to death with Christ ever anew. Then you will experience a glorious resurrection of the new man.

177

3

Always give thanks for everything to our God and Father in the name of our Lord Jesus Christ.
Eph. 5:20 LB

To give thanks at all times is the solution to all problems. Whoever gives thanks for everything will experience that even the hardest things are transformed, for in giving thanks, he sees that a treasure is contained in the cross — a gift of God's love. By giving thanks, we discover this hidden treasure.

4

See to it that no one pays back wrong for wrong, but always aim at doing the best you can for each other and for all men.
1 Thess. 5:15 NEB

Bear with special love those you find difficult to get along with and take care that not the faintest trace of vengeance is to be found in your thoughts and deeds. And in your sin and weakness you can be assured of God's special love.

5

Serve the Lord with fear, and rejoice with trembling.
Ps. 2:11 AV

In serving the Lord, let your one concern be to serve Him aright and to bring Him joy. Stand in holy fear lest you seek personal gratification in your activities and tasks in the Kingdom of God. Rejoice, but with trembling, when you are granted success. Only if you are solely concerned about Jesus, will your service be pure and devoid of mixed motives. Then it will bear eternal fruit.

6

Pray without ceasing. 1 Thess. 5:17 AV

Converse with God in love — not only during your prayer times, but every hour of the day. Even when you are very busy, the name of Jesus, the 'Jesus prayer', should be ringing in your heart, for great power lies in pronouncing His name in prayer. Let your whole life be a prayer. Then it will have been worth living, for through prayer great things are accomplished. In prayer you will be united with God Himself. Your heart will be strong, cheerful and immersed in peace, because you are one with His will.

7

Do good, and lend, expecting nothing in return; and your reward will be great, and you will be sons of the Most High; for he is kind to the ungrateful and the selfish. Luke 6:35

Do not forget to help and give gifts to those who forget you and overlook you. Then you will be a true child of the Father, who lets His sun shine on the good and the bad. And one day you will be able to share in the radiance of His glory, since you reflected His nature here below.

8

Encourage the fainthearted. 1 Thess. 5:14

The fainthearted and downcast, who are like a 'smouldering wick', should not be criticised, but rather encouraged. Paint them a picture of the victorious might of Jesus, which is greater than everything — yes, greater than all the fears and hardships that trouble one's heart. Comfort yourself in the same way when you feel like a 'smouldering wick', so that you can be a true comforter to others.

9

Do not resist one who is evil. But if any one strikes you on the right cheek, turn to him the other also.
Matt. 5:39

Though innocent, Jesus, the Lamb of God, endured wickedness for your sake and in love surrendered Himself to it of His own free will. So when others wrong you, follow Jesus, the Lamb, and do not retaliate, but bear wrongs in patient love. And as the 'bride of the Lamb' you will one day be raised to His throne, because you have done to others as Jesus did to you.

10

Do not fear what you are about to suffer.

Rev. 2:10a

Saying Yes to the cross takes away its power to crush us. So say Yes to the cross — even before it comes — and suffering will lose its power over you. The fear in your heart will be transformed into peace and assurance, and in the midst of suffering you will experience the presence of the Lord, His love and His comfort.

11

Since we have these promises, beloved, let us cleanse ourselves from every defilement of body and spirit, and make holiness perfect in the fear of God.

2 Cor. 7:1

In contrition cleanse your heart ever anew in the blood of Jesus. Then God will come and dwell in your heart. Along this path of purification you will attain God's great promises.

12

Do not say to your friend, 'Come back again; you shall have it tomorrow' — when you have it already.

Prov. 3:28 NEB

When a request is made of you, give of what you have without delay. Otherwise you may miss your opportunity to fulfil the request and thus disappoint not only the person who made the request, but Jesus. Whoever gives to others will receive gifts from God — both here and in eternity.

13

Be doers of the word, and not hearers only, deceiving yourselves.   Jas. 1:22

Beware of living in self-deception. The consequences are serious if we deceive ourselves. Examine yourself to see whether you have put into practice all that God says in His Word, His commandments and instructions. If you do not practise what you have heard, you will be counted among the hypocrites, whom Jesus threatens with a severe judgment, just as He conversely promises joy and blessing to those who are doers of the word.

14

Implore God's blessing on those who hurt you.
                                    Luke 6:28 LB

Even when it is hard for you, pray much for those who hurt and insult you. In this way you will learn to love them — and Jesus, who prayed for His enemies, will imprint His traits upon you and you will come close to Him.

15

God wants you to be holy and pure, and to keep
clear of all sexual sin ... If anyone refuses to live
by these rules he is not disobeying the rules of
men but of God who gives his Holy *Spirit to you.*
1 Thess. 4:3,8 LB

It is not left to your discretion to decide whether
pre-marital or extra-marital relations are permis-
sible or even good. It is not we who decide what is
good or bad, but God alone. And God says that
every marital relationship out of wedlock is sin, an
offence that incurs His judgment. Remember, he
who holds the living, holy God in contempt will
not go unpunished.

16

Would that you were cold or hot!   Rev. 3:15b

Is your heart lukewarm? If so, it is a sign that you
do not love Jesus, for love is ardent and fiery.
Jesus' primary concern is that we love Him. This
is the first and foremost commandment and Jesus'
greatest desire. If Jesus does not find this fervent
love in you, He laments over you. Therefore, repent
if there is lukewarmness in your heart, so that one
day you won't have to hear the words from Jesus'
lips, 'I do not know you.'

17

Do not yield your members to sin as instruments of wickedness. Rom. 6:13a

Let the Spirit of God convict you whenever you treat sin lightly in your life. For by toying with sin, you offer your bodily members to serve as instruments of Jesus Christ's Enemy, as weapons of evil in the battle between light and darkness. Consider what effect your attitude towards sin in everyday life has for the Kingdom of God. Sin destroys the Kingdom of God; repentance and contrition build it up.

18

Do not neglect to do good and to share what you have, for such sacrifices are pleasing to God. Heb. 13:16

Are acts of kindness and sharing your possessions just as important to you as your daily bread? Do you remember to do these things just as you would remember to attend to your most pressing needs? A life without sacrifice is spiritually dead. Make sacrifices, and streams of divine blessing will flow from your life.

19

Love each other with brotherly affection and take delight in honouring each other.   Rom. 12:10 LB

Do not belittle any person, but think highly of him. Practise showing respect to others not as a mere formality, but with a humble and loving heart. Then God will also think highly of you and one day you will be crowned with honour at His throne.

20

Thou shalt not steal.   Exod. 20:15 AV

Love is unable to harm others and deprive them of their possessions, for the loss would be painful to them. On the contrary, love desires to bestow gifts on others and enrich them. Whoever acts against love — taking for himself the possessions of others — has to suffer the consequences of his actions. Because of his sin he incurs the judgment of God. Even in this life he can see how ill-gotten gain does not bring prosperity or blessing. And on the day of judgment, which awaits every man, the penalty of God will come upon him without fail.

21

Whoever would draw near to God must believe that he exists and that he rewards those who seek him. Heb. 11:6b

Never say, 'I can't go on. I can't believe any longer.' For then you throw away the crown, which will be granted only to those who keep faith. Rather say, 'I will persevere, for You are alive, my Lord, and You see me and will not let me be tempted beyond my strength. I trust in You!'

22

Be at peace among yourselves. 1 Thess. 5:13b

Discord destroys family happiness and creates breaches in the Body of Christ. Peace builds up. Peace paves the way for the Kingdom of God to grow in our midst. What price have you paid to re-tie the bonds of unity and true peace?

23

Fight the good fight of faith. 1 Tim. 6:12a AV

By not fighting the battle of faith, we place ourselves in a dangerous position, for then the Enemy will soon have us in his clutches. So keep up the battle by continually hurling the promises of God at the Enemy in the unshakable conviction that they are yea and amen. Not with an ordinary prayer, in which you merely mention your requests to God, will you win the victory, but only by waging a life-or-death battle with the Enemy. So fight the good fight of faith!

24

Give to everyone who asks you. Luke 6:30 NEB

Open wide the door of your heart to everyone who comes to you and asks something of you. Leave no request unanswered, and God will open wide the door of His heart and graciously respond to your requests.

25

Don't give the Devil a chance. Eph. 4:27 GNB

Close the door to your heart whenever you hear a voice within you or without, making derogatory remarks about someone else. If you don't, you will let the Devil in. And then he will take up residence in your heart.

26

Be still before the Lord, and wait patiently for him.
Ps. 37:7

Even when the will of God is incomprehensible to you, accept it quietly, without rebelling. Trust that His will is good, since it has come from a heart of eternal love, the heart of your Father, who has only the best in mind for you. The more you surrender yourself to His will, the less painful the hardships will be to you. By willingly placing yourself under His mighty hand, you will be prepared for eternity. You will become humble and learn to wait in trust for the hour of God's help, which will never fail to come.

27

Thou shalt love the Lord thy God with all thy heart, and with all thy soul, and with all thy mind.
Matt. 22:37 AV

God is waiting for your love. An expression of your love is that you give Him everything that makes life worth living for you, that you place at His disposal all earthly possessions and gifts that are precious and dear to you and say, 'Take my life, my will, my wishes, my time and energy, my money and goods, my dear ones.'

Then you will experience how happy Jesus' love will make you. And moreover, He will give you a hundredfold in return, just as He promised to shower you with blessings.

28

Let us then pursue the things that make for peace.
Rom. 14:19 NEB

You do not build up the Kingdom of God when you insist upon your rights — instead, you destroy it. Insistence upon one's rights and quarrelling are

OCTOBER

enemies of God. So choose peace — even at the expense of your rights — and you will be God's friend.

29

Neither circumcision counts for anything nor uncircumcision, but keeping the commandments of God.   1 Cor. 7:19

One thing is of utmost importance for time and eternity. And that is to heed and obey the commandments of God. You will be judged one day according to your response to the commandments, for faith without works is dead in the eyes of God. He 'has created us for a life of good deeds' (Eph. 2:10 GNB).

God will one day judge us according to what we have done in our lives — whether it was good or evil. So let the commandments be your guide today.

30

Sing forth the honour of his name: make his praise glorious.   Ps. 66:2 AV

Great power lies in the name of Jesus. In singing and giving praise to His name, we break the might of the Enemy. Praise the name of Jesus greatly. In it you will find victory over all that oppresses you; you will find deliverance and assistance, balsam for your wounds and joy in all suffering.

31

Do all things without grumbling or questioning.
Phil. 2:14

The spirit of grumbling cost the people of Israel their entry into Canaan long ago. They reaped the fruit of their grumbling — forty hard years in the wilderness. So refrain from grumbling. It is not the hardship that befalls you, but your grumbling that makes you despair and feel that you are in the wilderness.

November

Every new Yes uttered in obedience
to God's commandments,
every act of commitment to Him
binds us closer to His heart.

1

Trust in him at all times, O people; pour out your heart before him; God is a refuge for us. Ps. 62:8

Never despair. Despair has never altered adversity, nor has it brought anyone through to victory. Trust and cling to the Lord. Then your difficulties will be transformed, and you will gain the victory.

2

Do not listen to an accusation against an elder unless it is brought by two or more witnesses.

1 Tim. 5:19 GNB

Regard those who have a leading position in the Body of Christ as worthy of honour. Therefore, if you hear any complaint against them, do not let it enter your heart unless it is confirmed by two or three witnesses. If you pay heed to the Accuser, you open the way for him to do his work of destruction in the Body of Christ.

3

My son, be attentive to my words; incline your ear to my sayings. Let them not escape from your sight; keep them within your heart. Prov. 4:20f.

Revere the commandments of God as words uttered by His mouth; ponder over them ever anew in your heart that they may accompany you through the day as His earnest request to you. They will bring you to contrition and thus drive you into the arms of Jesus when you find that you cannot fulfil them. Yes, they will cause you to praise the blood of the Lamb over your failings. Do this and you will experience that 'if the Son makes you free, you will be free indeed' — free to fulfil God's will and instructions.

4

Accept one another as Christ accepted us, to the glory of God.   Rom. 15:7 NEB

To accept one another in love is to open one's heart to the other person and accept him just as he is. If you accept your neighbour, God will accept you.

5

Thus says the Lord: 'Keep justice, and do righteousness, for soon my salvation will come, and my deliverance be revealed.'   Isa. 56:1

Take up the battle against sin in your life. In this way you will be a living testimony to the grace of Jesus' redemption and deliverance. In a world that is running headlong into destruction, since it no longer calls injustice and sin by their proper names, you will be able to testify that real joy and blessing are to be found in a life lived according to the commandments of God in the power of Jesus' redemption.

6

Don't associate with the brother whose life is undisciplined.   2 Thess. 3:6 JBP

Undisciplined living is sin. It is dishonouring to God. If your brother continues in such ways despite admonishments, he can be roused from his indifference only if you sever connections with him. If you love Jesus, you will obey His word and take this course in order to help your brother and to testify in the sight of the world that such a way of life is not in accordance with Jesus' commandments.

7

Whatsoever things are true, whatsoever things are honest, whatsoever things are just, whatsoever things are pure, whatsoever things are lovely, whatsoever things are of good report; if there be any virtue, and if there be any praise, think on these things.   Phil. 4:8 AV

Every virtue is a trait of Jesus Christ. Whoever yearns to be like Jesus will endeavour to attain virtues. The more you are transformed into His nature, the more power you will have to serve Him properly. So make the virtues of Jesus your aim. They will be granted to those who give their old selves up to death ever anew.

195

NOVEMBER

8

Beware! Be on your guard against greed of every kind.   Luke 12:15a NEB

Greed — wanting to attain something at all costs — is a dangerous craving. Every craving ruins a person's life and happiness. Ask the Lord to show you where greediness has crept into your life. Renounce it before God by laying at Jesus' feet all that you wrongly yearn for, and say, 'I no longer want it.' God your Father will then give you that which you really need and which will make you truly happy.

9

Run, then, in such a way as to win the prize.

1 Cor. 9:24 GNB

Don't be lazy. Run each day's race with all your might, so that at the end you will receive the victory wreath from God. Keep on running even when you have had a fall. The victory wreath is won by him who does not stay down, but always gets up again, grasps the banner of faith, and keeps on running in the assurance that Jesus is Victor!

10

Let the word of Christ dwell in you richly. Col. 3:16

The children of Israel literally let the Word of God dwell in their midst. They fastened it to their doorposts and bound it round their arms, so that it would be a constant reminder and guide for their everyday lives. What do you do to let the morning Bible reading guide and accompany you throughout the day and to remind yourself of that which you have heard in order to put it into practice?

11

Remember the words of the Lord Jesus, how he said, It is more blessed to give than to receive.

Acts 20:35 AV

Give ungrudgingly and with a glad heart the tithe of your income for the Kingdom of God. God loves cheerful givers who out of love for Him give their tithes, even if it costs them much at the time and others call it foolish. So act according to His commandment and God will open the windows of heaven and shower you with a rich blessing.

12

'Yet even now,' says the Lord, 'return to me with all your heart, with fasting, with weeping, and with mourning; and rend your hearts and not your garments.' Return to the Lord, your God, for he is gracious and merciful, slow to anger, and abounding in steadfast love, and repents of evil.

Joel 2:12 — 14a

Don't repent just once — but every day anew turn from your sinful ways, from actions, words and thoughts that are wrong. Every time you have had a fall, come as a weeping sinner to the cross of Jesus. Then God will revoke His punishment and pour out His grace upon you according to His abundant mercy. The blood of Jesus will cleanse you and you will learn to overcome your weak points more and more. So take up this offer of grace and return to the Lord.

13

Love does not keep a record of wrongs.

1 Cor. 13:5 GNB

You can love your neighbour only if you destroy the record of the other person's faults that you have been keeping in your heart. Blot it out, so that it is no longer legible. In other words, forget what the other person has done to you. Then you will be able to love him. And having truly forgiven him, you can be assured of God's forgiveness for yourself.

14

Don't be afraid of people's scorn or their slanderous talk.

Isa. 51:7 LB

Be willing to bear it when men taunt you and 'say all manner of evil against you' for Jesus' sake. Then you will belong to Jesus, who was despised and rejected more than anyone else, and you will be counted among the prophets and elect, who endured such afflictions. Look forward to heaven where you will be honoured as much as you were disgraced here below.

15

Unto God our Father be glory forever and ever.
Phil. 4:20 LB

Let your day be filled with adoration of God. Then you will be joining in with the angels whose service is unceasing adoration and you will have a foretaste of heaven here on earth. All earthly cares will flee as you praise God for who He is — the almighty Lord and loving Father.

16

Thou shalt not bear false witness against thy neighbour.
Exod. 20:16 AV

Whoever bears false witness against his neighbour is a liar, and, as such, will incur a severe judgment from God. So do not treat the matter lightly and place a person in a bad light by passing on unfavourable statements that haven't been proved. They could be lies. If you deprive someone of his good reputation, which may be of more value to him than his life, you could ruin his life as a result. And for this you would never be able to make amends.

17

*Put on the breastplate of faith and love, and for a
helmet the hope of salvation.*   1 Thess. 5:8

Every morning when you begin the day, let Jesus
gird you anew with the armour of faith. Pray for
a new spirit of faith, new love from His heart and
the hope in the eternal glory, which the Holy Spirit
can give. This will strengthen you and help you to
overcome in all your struggles and temptations
during the day. And that which you ask for will
be given to you.

18

*When you vow a vow to God, do not delay paying
it; for he has no pleasure in fools.*   Eccles. 5:4

Do you want to come to know God better as the
Father, who will never disappoint you, but always
grant you gifts in His love? Then do not disappoint
Him by withholding that which you have promised
to give Him. God gives Himself wholly to him who
gives himself wholly to God.

19

*Instruct those who are rich in this world's goods
not to be proud.*   1 Tim. 6:17 NEB

When earthly goods come into your possession,
heed Scripture's admonition and be wary of the
danger of becoming attached to earthly things and

filled with arrogance and pride because of all your possessions, which make you appear great in the sight of others. In the face of this danger pray that God will make you lowly; humble yourself according to Jesus' words, so that God may lift you up in His time.

20

Turn ye unto me, saith the Lord of hosts, and I will turn unto you.   Zech. 1:3 AV

Nothing can make us so joyful as true contrition and repentance. Not only does it cause us to turn away from our sinful lives, which only make us unhappy, but it drives us into the arms of God and brings forth new life and new love for Jesus. So pray for nothing so much as true repentance.

21

My son, do not regard lightly the discipline of the Lord, nor lose courage when you are punished by him. For the moment all discipline seems painful rather than pleasant; later it yields the peaceful fruit of righteousness to those who have been trained by it.   Heb. 12:5,11

If you encounter hardship, it is often in answer to your prayer that God would remould you into His image and let you reach the goal of glory. If there had been an easier way to this goal, God would have chosen it for you. So accept His chastenings in loving patience. They are the answer to your prayers and will bring you the greatest thing of all — eternal glory.

22

Forgive, and you will be forgiven. Luke 6:37b

Take care that you do not keep a record in your heart of any bad thing that was said or done to you. Forgive, and you will experience the most precious gift of grace: the Lord will not hold your sins against you, but forgive you.

23

Immorality and all impurity ... must not even be named among you. Eph. 5:3

Unlike other sins, sexual immorality and impurity defile our body. These sins shall be manifest on our resurrection body to our disgrace in the sight of the whole world. So flee from immorality — yes, from every word and conversation that is contaminated by it.

24

In this confidence let us hold on to the hope that we profess without the slightest hesitation.
Heb. 10:23 JBP

Even in the darkest days cling to the hope that you have professed and that you live for: that your entry into the City of God has been prepared for you by the sacrifice of Jesus Christ. This city of glory, which is the dwelling place of the over-comers, really does exist. Remember, the sufferings of this present time are not worth comparing with the glory that awaits you. So persevere.

25

But you, man of God ... pursue justice, piety, fidelity, love, fortitude, and gentleness.

1 Tim. 6:11 NEB

Pursuit entails making a special effort, sacrificing strength and denying oneself all manner of things in order to attain the goal and win the trophy. What have you sacrificed in the way of time and energy and other things for special times of prayer in order to attain more faith, love and patience?

26

Despise not thou the chastening of the Lord.

Heb. 12:5 AV

Value the chastenings of the Lord highly. Esteem them in the knowledge that they are the loving blows of God, which He deals His elect in order to mould them into the glory of His image. Whoever gives thanks amid tears for the heavenly Father's chastenings will experience that they achieve great things.

27

You are to be perfect, even as your Father in heaven is perfect. Matt. 5:48 LB

Do not be content with small aims of faith. Rather, take this challenge of Jesus as a firm promise. Pray for the highest of all gifts, for the gift of divine love. It is a never-ending love, for it is the chief attribute of God and therefore imperishable like God Himself. This love is to be yours.

28

I am the Lord your God . . . Open your mouth wide, and I will fill it. Ps. 81:10

Expect much from God and you will experience much goodness. Expect everything from God and you will experience His love and aid in all things. So open your mouth wide, open your heart wide and open your hands, for the hungry and thirsty will receive and empty hands will be filled.

29

Love your enemies. Matt. 5:44

Love your enemies as your friends. Love them with the love that Jesus is able to give you — and though as a sinner you are actually God's enemy, you will be His friend.

30

Take hold of eternal life. For to this you were called.   1 Tim. 6:12b NEB

We are to reach out for divine life, which comes from the heart of God, for it is imbued with His love, joy and peace. We need this life, so that we in turn may pass it on to others. Converse with Jesus in prayer. In close communion with Him you will partake of His eternal life. So draw near to Jesus and you will come to know Him better through His Word and through the help of the Holy Spirit. In this way you will be able to take hold of the eternal life that He offers to you.

December

Of all the stars of promise,
none shines so brightly
as the commandments of God.
The most glorious fulfilment
awaits those who abide by them.

1

Be kind to one another, tenderhearted.   Eph. 4:32

Use your tongue, which has been given to you by God, to speak kind and tenderhearted words, and one day you will hear merciful words from the lips of God.

2

If any man would come after me, let him deny himself and take up his cross and follow me.
Matt. 16:24

Take up your cross daily. You need it. It will not crush you. God has sent it to you in love to give you something good. It will draw you close to Jesus here on earth and prepare eternal glory for you. Indeed, it will bear you upwards to heaven. Knowing this, embrace your cross and bear it.

3

Do not despise prophesying.   1 Thess. 5:20

Do not despise that which Christians, empowered by God and inspired by the Holy Spirit, speak or prophesy. If you do so, you despise God's words. Then you may suddenly experience that your heart can no longer take in or understand the Word of God properly and that you lose your living relationship to Him.

DECEMBER

4

Walk ye in all the ways that I have commanded you, that it may be well unto you. Jer. 7:23b AV

There is only one way that ends in the City of God and that is the path trodden in obedience to the will of God. So follow your short path here on earth as a true disciple of Jesus in obedience to the commandments of God, the declaration of His will — and you will taste His goodness here on earth and one day enter the City of God.

5

Never avenge yourselves. Leave that to God, for he has said that he will repay those who deserve it. Rom. 12:19 LB

Whoever avenges himself for the evil done to him binds God's hands, so that He cannot come to our defence as He has promised to when we suffer unfair treatment. So do not avenge yourself. Otherwise, you make it impossible for the mighty God to intervene on your behalf.

6

Speak to one another with the words of psalms, hymns and sacred songs. Eph. 5:19 GNB

What do we talk to each other about? That which fills our hearts. Out of the heart of a spiritual person come spiritual songs, hymns and psalms. What comes from your lips?

7

Yahweh Sabaoth, the God of Israel, says this: Amend your behaviour and your actions and I will stay with you here in this place. Jer. 7:3 JB

You can amend your behaviour only when you repent and turn to God. So turn from your sinful ways ever anew and you will be happy, for God is close to those who turn to Him in contrition. And what joy could be greater than God turning to us and granting us His love!

8

Have no anxiety about anything, but in everything by prayer and supplication with thanksgiving let your requests be made known to God. Phil. 4:6

Jesus not only forbids worrying, which is a pagan attitude, but through the Apostles He shows us a way to deal with the mountains of cares and worries that loom before us. Turn every problem into a prayer. Indeed, when faced with insurmountable obstacles, praise God that He is Lord and thank Him in advance for having prepared a way out and having help in store for you — and you will experience His aid.

9

Fear God and obey his commandments, for this is the entire duty of man. For God will judge us for everything we do, including every hidden thing, good or bad. Eccles. 12:13f. LB

Are you looking for happiness and joy? Then obey the commandments of God. They bring divine life and thus peace and joy to those who abide by them, since they come from God Himself, who is Life.

10

On every Lord's Day each of you should put aside something from what you have earned during the week, and use it for this offering. The amount depends on how much the Lord has helped you earn. 1 Cor. 16:2 LB

Your income and salary are not meant solely for you and your family. God, who gave it to you, raises His rightful claim to it, asking you to give part of it to Him for His kingdom and the Body of Christ. Do this and you will experience that He will richly reward you and bless and increase your money.

11

Purify yourselves, you who bear the vessels of the Lord. Isa. 52:11

To stand in the Lord's service is to perform a holy service; it means being called to be a fellow worker with God, upon whom He makes special demands. So apply God's holy standard to yourself. Be prepared to come before the holiness of God every day anew and let your life, nature and deeds be purified in the fire of His judgment and cleansed by the blood of the Lamb. Such purification by judgment and grace empowers your life, words and service, and you will be privileged to call many to God.

12

Be still before the Lord. Ps. 37:7

Only in quiet waters does God cast His anchor. God only draws near to a soul that enters quietness, a soul whose thoughts and feelings have been stilled. So avoid all noisy behaviour and speech, for they drive away the presence of God. Let everything be still within you — and if possible around you. And God will incline Himself to you and speak with you.

13

Do not grumble against God, as some of them did.
1 Cor. 10:10 NEB

If you are in a spiritual wilderness, don't grumble as the children of Israel did. Otherwise, you will perish in the wilderness. Believe, like Moses, that God gives manna in the wilderness, quails and water. Then you will be refreshed in the wilderness and will reach Canaan both here and above.

14

Command them in the name of the Lord not to argue over unimportant things. 2 Tim. 2:14 LB

Avoid all arguments and disputes, for they destroy paradise, the kingdom of love. Be peace-loving and a peacemaker. Then you will pave the way for the Kingdom of God, which is a kingdom of peace. And as a child of the Father you will rest in peace in His arms.

15

Seek the Lord and his strength, seek his presence continually. Ps. 105:4

God has first right to your love and your time. Give Him your time, so that you may converse with Him in love. He is waiting for you to inquire of Him and seek Him first of all, bringing all your requests before His countenance. Then you will experience what it is to be restored by the light of His countenance.

16

Tend the flock of God that is your charge ... not as domineering over those in your charge but being examples to the flock. 1 Pet. 5:2f.

The staff of meekness was the staff with which Jesus shepherded His flock. If you want to lead difficult people in such a way that they can fit in with the church or the group entrusted to your care, treat them with meekness. By the testimony and example of your life you will overcome even hard hearts.

17

Thou shalt not covet thy neighbour's house, thou shalt not covet thy neighbour's wife, nor his manservant, nor his maidservant, nor his ox, nor his ass, nor any thing that is thy neighbour's.
Exod. 20:17 AV

To covet that which belongs to others is to set foot on forbidden territory. By doing so, you will have wandered into Satan's domain and be at the mercy of his temptations as Eve was. The longer she gazed at the tree with the forbidden fruit, the greater her desire grew. This led her to take the step of disobedience, and Satan achieved his objective. As a result Eve incurred the punishment of God. Therefore, say before God and man, 'I desire nothing but that which God has ordained for me and given me.' Only then will you find blessing and satisfaction, and the Enemy will yield.

18

Whatever you wish that men would do to you, do so to them.　　　　　　　　　　Matt. 7:12

Treat others in the same way as you would like to be accepted, treated and spoken to. Then you will fulfil the first commandment — the commandment to love the Lord your God with all your heart, soul and mind and to love your neighbour as yourself. This commandment has God's promise of blessing.

19

Glorify God in your body.　　　　　　　1 Cor. 6:20

You have been redeemed, that your whole life — including your body and its members — may praise God and glorify Him in the sight of man. A pure life glorifies God and testifies to Him, the Holy One. Choose this pure life, so that you will not disgrace Jesus. Do it in thanksgiving for His redemption.

20

Love believes all things, hopes all things.

1 Cor. 13:7

Love cannot do otherwise than continue to believe for others, even when no change can be seen in them, for an attribute of love is that it never ceases until its objective has been achieved and the other person has been helped. Measure your love for your neighbour according to this standard, even if he is hard for you to bear.

21

Humble yourselves therefore under the mighty hand of God, that he may exalt you in due time.

1 Pet. 5:6 AV

If you humble yourself under the hand of God when He chastens you, the hour will come when the same hand that lay heavily upon you will draw you to His heart in great mercy. For God is a Father, who loves you, His child, and when He strikes you, it is only with compassion. When He has achieved His objective with you by means of His chastening, His heart will overflow with goodness, which He had to hold back for your well-being. Indeed, He will show you even more goodness than before.

DECEMBER

22

*Offer to God a sacrifice of thanksgiving, and pay
your vows to the Most High.* Ps. 50:14

God the Father, who has a heart of love, yearns
for His children to show Him the response of their
love, which is thanksgiving. Don't disappoint Him
by thanking Him only with your lips while your
life speaks of ingratitude because you do not give
Him your will and your time and do not obey His
commandments. Commit your whole life to the
Father in thanksgiving and you will know the
fullness of His love.

23

*Bless, for to this you have been called, that you
may obtain a blessing.* 1 Pet. 3:9

Whenever you meet someone — whoever it may
be and wherever it may be — let your greeting be
a blessing. And God will bless you from heaven in
return.

24

*Rejoice in the Lord always; again I will say, Re-
joice.* Phil. 4:4

Yes, in the darkest times rejoice that one joy cannot be taken away from you — the joy that you
have a Friend in Jesus Christ, who like a never-
setting sun illuminates all darkness. He came in

the depths of night and as a tiny child made His bed in a manger so as to bring light to this dark world. So let Jesus, the Sun of joy, shine into your heart. Then the depths of your darkness will become light and you will be comforted in your sadness.

25

Ascribe to the Lord the glory due his name; bring an offering.   Ps. 96:8

God has a right to our sacrifices, for He sacrificed that which was dearest to Him, His beloved Son. So do not deny Him sacrifices. The more you love Him, the more you will rejoice in making sacrifices.

26

Let your speech always be gracious, seasoned with salt, so that you may know how you ought to answer every one.   Col. 4:6

Take care that the salt of love is not missing from your words and actions. It is like a nugget of gold that will weigh much when your words and deeds are weighed in eternity. So take care that it be found in all that you say and do.

DECEMBER

27

This commandment we have from him, that he who loves God should love his brother also.

1 John 4:21

In loving God, we come into a very close relationship with Him. This union with Jesus will make you like Him, and He is Love. He demonstrated His love, however, by loving all men. So seek fellowship with Jesus; spend quiet hours communing with Him in love and you will be constrained to love your brother too.

28

Seek the Lord while he may be found, call upon him while he is near.   Isa. 55:6

Do not neglect on any day to come to God through the open door of prayer. Today it is still open. Give thanks for this. But remember that it can be closed without your realising it if for a long time you have been indifferent and have neglected to inquire after God or have persisted in pride and other sins. So seek the Lord daily and He will answer you daily.

29

Seek the things that are above.   Col. 3:1

Whenever the things of this world seek to captivate your mind and intellect, tear your thoughts away from them and set your mind on your eternal home. Bring whatever you see during the day into relationship with God and immerse it in eternity. Then you will find it again in eternity as a blessing.

30

Make the best possible use of your time.
Col. 4:5 JBP

Make the most of this day. It will never return. But that which you put into it in the way of thoughts, prayers and deeds you will find again in eternity. So take care that you put in much love, faith and prayer, and you will have a rich harvest above.

31

Commit to the Lord all that you do, and your plans will be fulfilled.
Prov. 16:3 NEB

God has a wonderful plan for our lives and is leading us along a path that is suited to our strength and abilities. So do not refuse to let Him be the Architect of your life. Be willing to do whatever is required of you. In obedience to God's leadings, accept the bricks that He gives you. Lay them into the building of your life day by day — and a wonderful building will rise up.

ACKNOWLEDGEMENTS

From the variety of English Bible translations available today, each verse was selected in order to convey the meaning presented in the corresponding verses from the German Bible translations, which were used in the original German edition of *More Precious than Gold*.

Scripture quotations not otherwise identified are taken from the *Revised Standard Version of the Bible,* copyrighted 1946 and 1952, © 1971 and 1973, by the Division of Christian Education of the National Council of the Churches of Christ in the USA, and used by permission.

Scripture quotations identified AV are taken from the King James Version of the Bible, published by the Syndics of the Cambridge University Press, London.

Scripture quotations identified NEB are taken from *The New English Bible,* copyrighted 1961 and 1970 by the Delegates of the Oxford University Press and the Syndics of the Cambridge University Press, and used by permission.

Scripture quotations identified AB are taken from *The Amplified Bible,* Old Testament, Copyright © 1962, 1964, Zondervan Publishing House, and used by permission.

Scripture quotations identified LB are taken from *The Living Bible,* © 1971, Tyndale House Publishers, and used by permission.

Scripture quotations identified JBP are taken from J.B. Phillips: *The New Testament in Modern English,* Revised Edition (© J.B. Phillips 1958, 1960, 1972).

Scripture quotations identified GNB are taken from the *Good News Bible* —Old Testament: Copyright © American Bible Society 1976, New Testament; Copyright © American Bible Society 1966, 1971, 1976, and used by permission.

Scripture quotation identified GNMM is taken from *Good News for Modern Man,* Fontana Books, 1968, © American Bible Society, 1966.

Scripture quotations identified JB are taken from *The Jerusalem Bible,* copyrighted 1966 by Darton, Longman & Todd, Ltd. and Doubleday & Company, Inc.

Cover photo: *Weidenroschen mit Sonne,* used by permission of Hugo Schottle, Wurzbach, West Germany.

The Blessings of Illness; $1.50

"Just as illnesses differ from one another, so our need for comfort varies with each illness . . . . Jesus can transform every trial and trouble into blessing." Mother Basilea meditates upon the Lord's leadings, which bring us blessings in the most unexpected ways.